Play With Me

I tried to teach my child from books;
He gave me only puzzled looks.
I tried to teach my child with words;
they passed him by, oft unheard.
Despairingly I turned aside;
"How shall I teach this child!" I cried.
Into my hand he put the key;
"Come" he said, "play with me."

Author Unknown

SensorySecrets How to Jump-Start Learning In Children

Copyright © 2001	Catherine Chemin Schneider
2nd Printing	2006
Senior Editor	Pat Benton
Copy Editors	Jodi King
	Mary Alice Hill
Cover Illustration & Graphic Design	Daniel Potter

*This book is dedicated to my extraordinary husband, **Dan**, who believes in me and continues to support my dream of helping children throughout the world!*

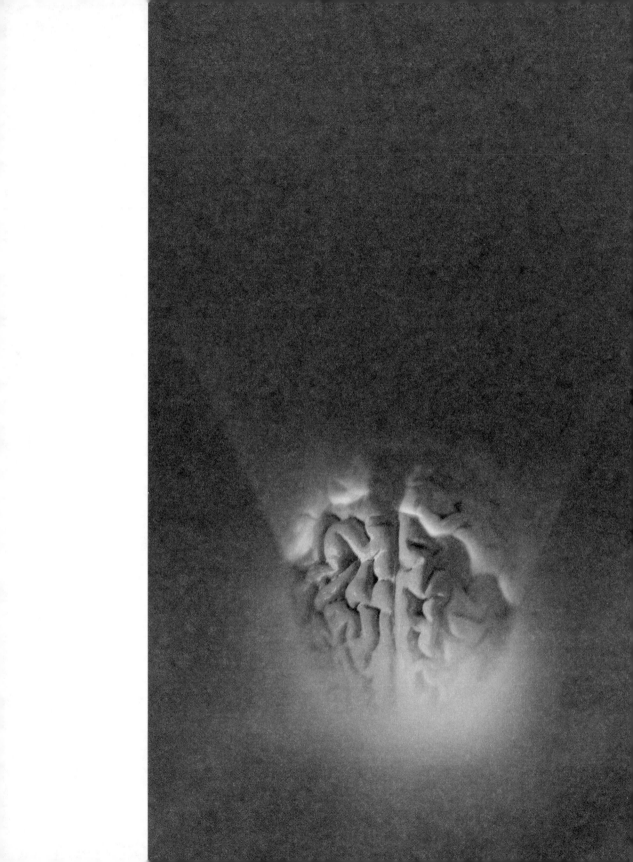

Contents

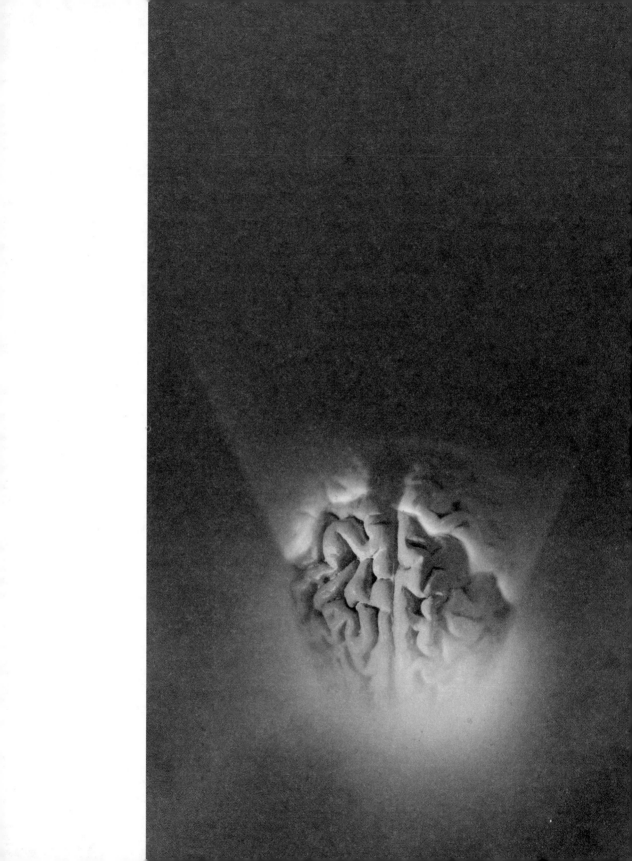

cknowlegements

Dr. A.J. Ayres began working with the theory of sensory integration in the late 1950's. To her we all owe a debt of gratitude.

Thank you to my parents, Irma and Tony Chemin, who believe that their daughters can do anything they put their minds to. To my husband, Dan Schneider, and to my sister-in-law and friend, Carol Poltorak, who gave me much-needed encouragement to reach my goal, and who spent countless hours proofreading the manuscript. To Dr. Arlene Taylor for the generous gift of consultation on the manuscript. To Patti Schneider, our daughter, a gifted occupational therapist, who used every minute of her free time to help in the revision of the Foundational Skills Inventory. To our son, David Schneider, and to Cheryl Appel for much-needed computer consultation.

To Russ Potter, my publisher, who is one in a million, and who truly follows the mission of helping mankind to share Concerned Communications. To Pat Benton, my patient, kind, and loving editor who had the monumental job of transferring countless pages of technical information into a readable, action-focused message. To Jodi King, my lifeline to sanity in the world of grammar and in fine-tuning the manuscript. To Daniel Potter, my expert in layout and design.

To my dear friends Carole Mullins, Darlene Bublin, Anne Hill, Donna Del Favero, and Sachiko Sunami for collaborating and supporting me with much-needed positive energy and love throughout this project. To Lynn Armitage for consulting and collaborating on the manuscript, as well as improving upon and creating new graphics. To Barb Wright and her staff for patience, encouragement, and help with binding the manuscript in the early stages of publishing.

Thank you to all of the gracious people I continue to meet in my work, and at the airport in transit from one workshop or seminar to another. You've shared your wisdom, stories, and questions to help us meld minds and seek to determine why we make the choices that we do. We spend days, hours—or sometimes just a few seconds—together. Often when you walk away thanking me, I, too, have a grateful heart, since the time we've shared broadened our insight on how to alter decisions that seemed inevitable before we met. My life and understanding have been blessed by our encounters, and I want to thank all of you for making the pages of this book *real*. You helped me to apply this potent information to all of life, rather than only to the situations that I encounter in my work with children in educational settings.

As we move to the second printing, I would again like to thank all my friends at The Concerned Group for their outstanding commitment to this powerful message! Together we are changing lives: one step at a time!

Notes From the Author

Research about sensory integration dysfunction is ongoing and subject to interpretation. What we know about this subject may change with time. Readers with concerns about the neurological development of children are advised to consult a qualified professional. Neither the author nor the publisher takes responsibility for actions by persons reading this book or the misapplication of concepts presented herein.

Because this is a universal subject that affects people of both genders, throughout *Sensory Secrets* masculine and feminine pronouns are used alternately. I hope that this enables the important message of the book to flow effectively.

Although the anecdotes and experiences related in this book are real, names have been changed to protect the confidentiality of all concerned.

—*Catherine Chemin Schneider*

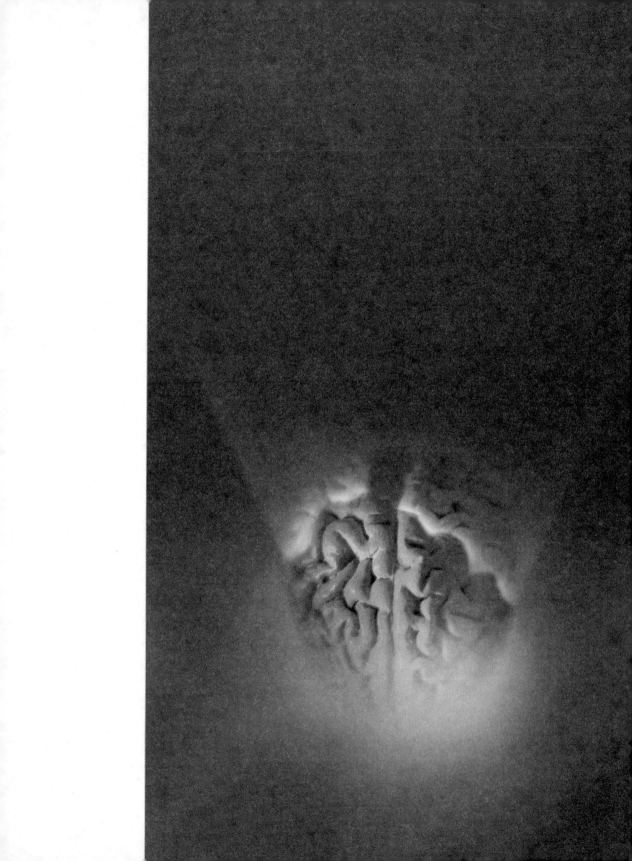

Introduction

Sensory Secrets: How to "Jump-start" Learning in Children will help you to understand how children learn. Exciting information about the importance of sensory motor processing/sensory integration needs to be tied together and made practical and understandable. This book may be the "missing link" in helping you to understand the foundation skills for all learning.

Simply stated, you probably already know what to do to create a firm foundation for children to learn. This includes the basics:

- Play with your children, dance with them, imagine, and see the wonder of the world as they see it. Move, grow, and learn with them.

- Hold your children; feel the texture of the universe with them. Taste, smell, and look at all of the choices around you. Some of the best things in life are experiences that are taken for granted until they're gone forever.

- Read to them, opening the world of knowledge and understanding. Make time to listen to them as they read to you and discover the magic and metaphor of fairy tales, where the unreal is obvious.

- Listen to your children. Actively repeat the message they're giving you to make sure you understand what they're saying. Talk to them using the tone in your voice to convey the love that you have for them.

- Carefully watch and learn from the actions of your children. Use their behavior as a form of secret communication that often speaks louder than words. Pay close attention to the tone of voice and the body language that they use when they do talk to you. You will gain a great deal of information for the time invested.

Somewhere deep down inside we already know these things. Yet it is also obvious that these basics are not being emphasized. Many parents and educators believe that in order to help our children be the best they can be requires a sophisticated approach to learning with emphasis on academics at earlier and earlier stages of development. Because of this philosophy, the necessity for movement, touch, taste, smell, the use of sight and hearing must be understood and brought again into the forefront.

What seems on the surface to be simple—that all learning has its basis in sensory development—is actually rooted in complex neurology. In earlier eras mastering the basics was accomplished automatically within the daily life experience of growing up the "old-fashioned" way. With increasing dependence upon technology, our ways of moving and sensing our world have changed. The automatic development of the skills necessary to create a firm foundation for learning has been short-circuited. In this process, we have also become programmed to feel less and less.

This book is based on the belief that children need movement and stimulation of the sensory systems in order to facilitate the learning process and that the opportunity for these seems to be diminishing in our society as we continue to move toward technology. The need for movement and the quantity and type of stimulation to the sensory systems differ among children, even as they do among adults. The differing needs are based on a whole range of factors including gender, sensory preference, level of introversion/extroversion, and thinking style. Nevertheless, there are some general principles—related to movement and to stimulation of the sensory systems—and it is these that we will address.

Understanding this information can help our children to learn more easily and quickly. They can be happier and heathier when learning requires less effort.

Children in educational settings have taught me what I am about to share with you. Working with them—along with physicians, parents, educators, therapists and administrators—helped me to realize that we all learn from each other. People with special needs are our finest "teachers." They are in our lives, and we are better because of them. I'm taking the lessons that I have gleaned from them and sharing them with you.

Throughout this book you'll come across terms that may be unfamiliar to you. These technical phrases (printed in italics) may be useful when talking with a professional about your child. Many of them are included in the glossary.

The sometimes subtle changes in the way children process information is the crux of this book. These patterns are shaping our children today. Come with me and discover how our youngsters learn.

—*Catherine Chemin Schneider*

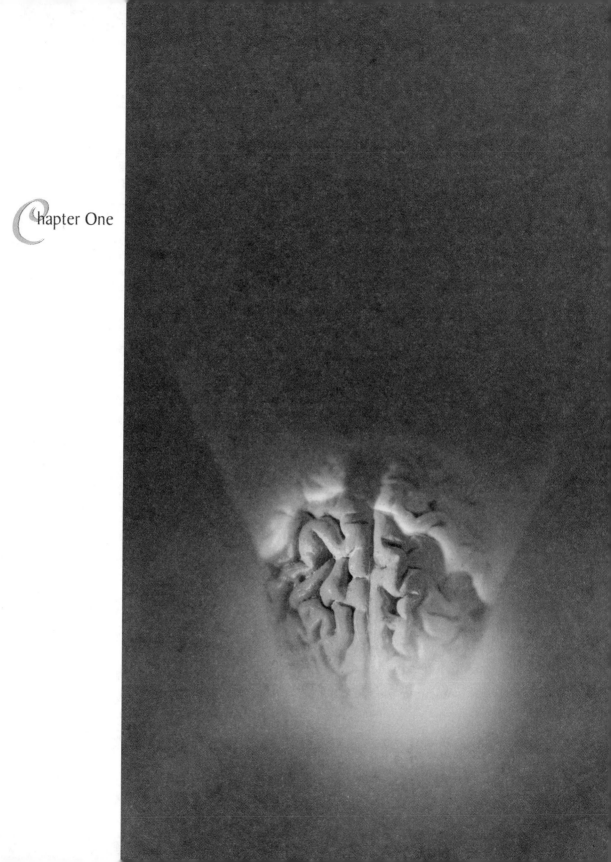

Chapter One

ake-up Call
Slow Down…You Grow too Fast

America, this book is a wake-up call! Choose to ignore its message, and negative forces will continue to permeate our lives. Choose to respond to it, and it may help to restore the health and well-being of our children.

Our busy schedules leave us little time for the study of child development. Through this book, I'm offering an opportunity for you to see clearly how this lack of understanding is impacting our youth. You can change this trend and respond with informed, enlightened decisions to make a positive difference.

Now is the time to understand the early development of the nervous system. Now is the time to grab hold of the answers that are right before our eyes. Now is the time to embrace the developmental information to be presented. This information is logical, and much of it is simple to apply. The call is right here—right now—to make the time you have with your children (and your own free time) the best it can be!

I like to identify information that comes in from the senses (seeing, hearing, smelling, touching, tasting, and muscle and joint sense) as "foundational," because the ability to use this necessary information creates the foundation for future learning and decision-making processes. Learning about this foundation is important and interesting, and it aids in understanding our own personal choices.

The practical application of this information can help our children, as well as ourselves. This book is not highly theoretical.

Other authors help us understand the complex neuroanatomy and neurochemistry that are involved in this complicated process; many of these are included in the bibliography. It is my goal to help you get a feel for the importance of this information and how it affects every person. My secondary goal is to motivate you to seek out additional information.

The ability to detect and use information that reaches us through our senses is called *sensory motor processing*. This taking in and making sense of what is seen, heard, touched, smelled, tasted, and felt—along with chemical changes caused by sensory processing—provides us with the ability to understand what is going on in our lives. This ability is critical, because it sets the stage for the learning process that provides our lives with meaning and direction.

Most young children use body movement to explore by touching, feeling, and organizing the sensory information they receive. We allow this ability to explore and sense to go on unceasingly as long as the child is considered an infant or toddler.

Then a child turns five. For some reason, we think she no longer needs to explore and sense. We seem to think that he is magically ready for school. The school experience includes huge doses of academics, with diminished time for exploring and sensing. In some parts of the country, recess is being made optional and/or being omitted from the school curriculum! The precious part of the day needs to be renamed—NLT (Neurodevelopmental Learning Time). It represents an important part of the day that gives children opportunities to be creative and make choices and decisions during supervised, unstructured, group play. We think that immersion in academics (with the exclusion of sensory exploration) will speed a child's readiness for the more advanced and complicated lessons of the future. Remember, play is "work" for children.

This fallacy includes the rationale that the earlier young children are exposed to academics—reading, writing, and arithmetic—the sooner they will exhibit the genius that is within. This also includes the belief that they will then forge onward to bigger and better things, regardless of their developmental ability to do so.

Hence, our children are being rushed out of experiences that create a firm foundation for learning. This foundation includes a balanced life of learning—drawing, singing, dancing, playing, creating, working, and thinking. Perhaps most importantly, it means that children should always be experiencing the wonder of life! They're being cheated out of the importance of moving, touching, and sharing.

Our children are suffering—not prospering—because of the brushing aside of these all-important foundational skills. The consequences are now being seen. It's time we look at our children from a different point of view.

Mastery of reading, writing, and arithmetic form our academic essentials but are not really "the basics" from which learning takes place. Physical education, recesses, unstructured play time, and practice/repetitive work help provide the basics and are being minimized.

It's little wonder that many of our children aren't producing legible handwriting! In many cases, they're not "writing" the letters—they're attempting to draw them. Drawing implies making the picture once, but serious handwriting education includes proper instruction, followed by repetition of the same letter(s) over and over. Proper letter shaping takes time and practice.

Foundational skills usually develop automatically during

the time that children play, explore their environment, and make up their own games and activities. Children of my generation (yes, I'm a Baby Boomer) spent their free time playing jacks, red rover, statues, red light-green light, Mother may I?, hide-and-seek, four square, and double Dutch jump rope.

Even if you didn't grow up on these simple outdoor activities, think about the process—all of them involved settling on the game to be played, gathering enough people to play, structuring the rules so that everyone understood them, and then actually playing the game for the fun of it! It demanded sharing, taking turns, and using sensory systems to develop skills that would be used for a lifetime. It was everything that we learned in kindergarten—and it was the best of life skills that we would take into adulthood!

The skills that develop the foundation for learning involve moving, feeling our bodies react to the pull of gravity on our muscles, touching, smelling, tasting, hearing a variety of voices, using a variety of voice intonations to influence meaning, talking with a variety of sounds, and so forth. As children learn the skills in patterns of repetition that are fun, their foundation for the future is laid.

Today's "programmed" children may not know how to occupy themselves; many are becoming accustomed to living in front of a screen (TV, computer, or arcade) or are being driven to a class, sports practice, or other planned activity or entertainment. Increasingly they're being cheated of experiences that have multidimensional opportunities, such as the simple playground activities mentioned above.

Parents with myriad responsibilities have an intuitive sense that individualized time with their children is important and necessary, and thus making every minute count for "quality" time is a goal. The question is, how can parents and grandparents make this precious time fun yet still significant in a child's development?

In the book *Your Miracle Brain,* Jean Carper shares dramatic scientific evidence in the field of brain research. One very important finding reveals a study done by William T. Greenough, of the University of Illinois at Urbana-Champaign in which rats were raised in three different environments (alone, two to a cage, and in groups with a playground atmosphere). Findings revealed that "Within only four days of exposure to the 'Disney wonderland of fun and games' the rats' brains went wild with new growth....Janice Juraska, neuroscientist at the University of Illinois, calls such experiments 'a unique demonstration of the power of the environment to sculpt the brain.' The implications for young children are mind-boggling."[1]

Once the foundation of all learning is understood, it's important to see why these basic skills are so important. Seemingly simple but complicated functions—based in intricate neurological development—play their roles. So let's move on to some greatly simplified basics of neurological development.

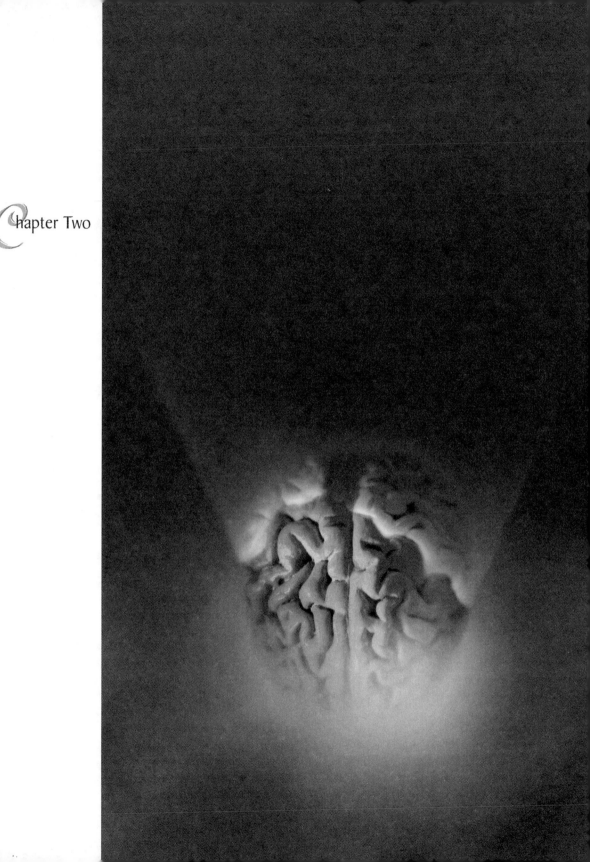

Chapter Two

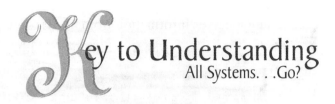ey to Understanding
All Systems. . .Go?

The central nervous system is composed of the brain and spinal cord. *Sensory motor processing* is a normal part of brain function—a complicated process that involves becoming aware of sensations and then organizing, storing, and retrieving that information which makes it possible to give meaning to what's been taken in. Sensory motor processing/sensory integration includes the ability to make sense of and to organize the vast amounts of information that enter the brain at the same time.

This processing and organizational ability is the foundation for motor skills, social behaviors, and the ability to accomplish more complicated tasks learned in school. It's important to learn about the sensory systems in order to understand how immature systems affect learning on a higher level. Difficulty with sensory processing tends to hide other abilities, which then have a hard time surfacing on their own.

The brainstem's filtering system (*reticular formation*) is a factor in determining whether information is noticed or ignored. (See Figure 1: Brain Anatomy, page 25.) The *brain stem* is like a relay station for the senses: touch, movement, and muscle/joint sense. The data received and transmitted help us to feel safe, to focus, and to keep our attention on the desired task. It also allows us to move without being fearful, and to use our body in an automatic fashion.

The top part of the brain—the *cortex*—is where higher-level thinking occurs. The back section of the brain is the *cerebellum*. The cerebellum receives information from muscles and joints, as seen in activities that involve pushing, pulling, stretching, lifting, carrying, tugging, grasping, squeezing, jumping, dancing, and wrestling.

The *vestibular system* (See Figure 2; level two, page 27 and Figure 3: Anatomy of the Inner Ear, page 28) has its receptors in the inner ear and senses movement of the head. The information processed by the vestibular system helps us to have an awareness of body position, and where we are in space (our relationship to gravity), how fast/slow we're going, in what direction we're traveling, and if we're still moving. It contains the *semicircular canals*, which detect angular movement, and the *utricle* and *saccule*, which detect linear movement and gravity.

The *somatosensory system—tactile system* (Figure 2; level three, page 27) includes receptors located in and under the skin. This system helps us to locate the edges of our body—where it ends—and helps us to be able to tell light-touch from heavy-touch sensations. Light touch alerts the protective portion of the system to be aware of the possibility of danger. Have you ever felt the light touch of a plant leaf on your head when you were sitting at a restaurant? Do you remember the second you felt it and how you quickly waved your arm around to check out the threatening feeling?

Unexpected light touch can poke at or move hair on the body. It can feel like an insect crawling on you and will usually get your attention. Heavy or pressure touch is familiar and predictable, soothing or comforting, smooth and/or warm. An example is firm stroking—as in a back rub.

The *proprioceptive system* (Figure 2; system intertwining with levels two and three, page 27) has receptors in joints, muscles, and tendons. As we use our bodies, we create contraction

Figure 1: Brain Anatomy

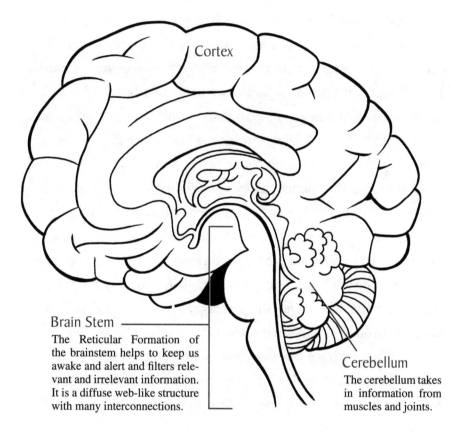

Cortex

Brain Stem ——————
The Reticular Formation of
the brainstem helps to keep us
awake and alert and filters rele-
vant and irrelevant information.
It is a diffuse web-like structure
with many interconnections.

Cerebellum
The cerebellum takes
in information from
muscles and joints.

and stretching of muscles and compression of joints. This data is constantly going to the brain to help us to know where we are in space and what we are doing with our body so that we don't have to pay attention to what our body is doing while we are concentrating on something else.

Sensory systems help us concentrate on the task at hand with the appropriate level of alertness. If any of these systems are immature—or have deficits—we'll compensate to gain the balance we need.

Here are some common examples of compensation. As a child, did you chew on your pencil while you were concentrating on what the teacher was saying? Do you like to eat tart candy to keep you alert when you have to focus on the details of a movie? Do you chew gum to stay awake during a lecture? Does sucking a thick milk shake through a straw calm you down? Do you fidget with the cord while talking on the phone? Do you sit with your legs crossed and bounce one slightly? The action of accomplishing one or more of these activities helps the system to focus and stay on task. These are strategies that may be used to help focus and function at an optimum level. (You may wish to refer to an excellent book cited in the bibliography by Williams and Shellenberger, *"How Does Your Engine Run?" A Leader's Guide to the Alert Program for Self-Regulation.*)

When we have too many malfunctioning, poor, or immature areas in our foundational skills, major problems surface. If the foundation is too weak, life can be difficult to manage.

Figure 2: The Key To Understanding

Figure 2: The Key To Understanding is an attempt to present a metaphor, a type of whole "picture" of a person with the necessary personal maturation elements needed to make learning happen in the intended automatic fashion. It is acknowledged that this is a gross simplification of complicated and intricate neurological information.

The center of the circle represents the core of the individual. Systems and skills radiate from this center level outward. Sensory information has a ripple effect; what happens at one level spreads to the other levels.

The top of each circle identifies technical terminology while the bottom of the same circle indicates the daily language equivalent.

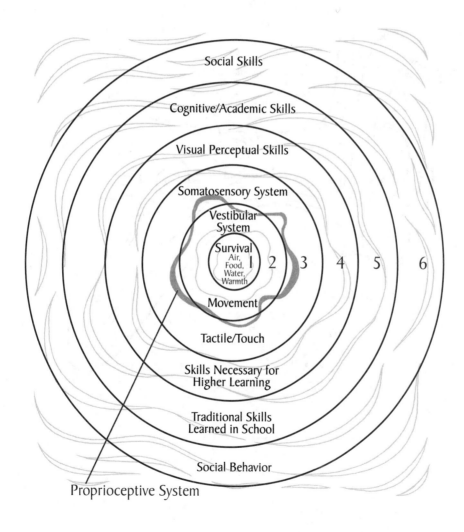

Social Skills

Cognitive/Academic Skills

Visual Perceptual Skills

Somatosensory System

Vestibular System

Survival
Air, Food, Water, Warmth

1 2 3 4 5 6

Movement

Tactile/Touch

Skills Necessary for Higher Learning

Traditional Skills Learned in School

Social Behavior

Proprioceptive System

Figure 3: Anatomy of the Inner Ear

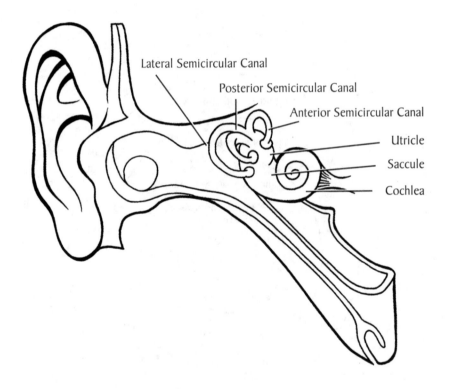

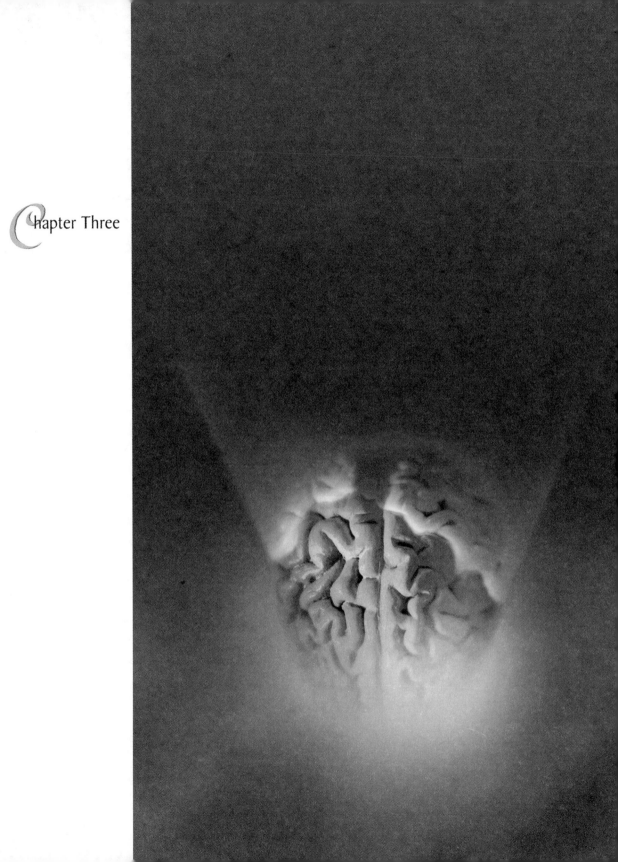

Chapter Three

ℱoundational Skills
Necessary for a Productive Life

A firm foundation is necessary to create the best opportunity for learning. And that foundation is based on what is taken in by the sensory systems—even before birth! The brain has many functions. These include:

- *Motor skills* (using your body's muscles to move and accomplish purposeful activity)

- *Cognitive skills* (using your brain for higher learning involved in academics)

- *Emotions* (signals to get your attention and give you information.)

- *Control of the autonomic nervous system* (that part of your brain that takes care of breathing, digestion, heart function, liver function etc.; if we had to think consciously of maintaining life we would certainly have very little time to do anything else!)

- *Sensory integration* (organizing all the information that comes in through the senses)

When there is a challenge in any one of these areas, it affects all the others.

Sensory motor processing/sensory integration is a process that involves the brain's ability to make sense and organize information that is being presented—all at once!—so that it can be used appropriately. This ability to process all that life throws at us is the foundation for the development of motor skills, social skills, and academic achievement. When there are malfunctions in these systems, energy that needs to be dedicated to complicated tasks is diverted to areas that are usually developed in early childhood.

When a child moves about, he is learning balance, using the eyes and body muscles together to sense how objects relate to each other in space, and increasing the tone of the muscles. When a young child is kept in the same positions and is deprived of movement and touch, the systems that are necessary for optimal learning are being short-changed.

None of us is perfect, and we all have holes in our foundations, places where we have challenges based in sensory processing. This has nothing to do with intelligence.

As adults, we compensate for these holes in our foundation by sidestepping that which is difficult. For example, if it is hard to do math, we'll use a calculator. If it's hard to read a map, we'll ask for directions that include written information. If we cannot translate digital information—say from a clock—to make sense to us, we'll buy analog clocks that give us a "picture" of time on the face of the clock. If we do better listening (auditory learner) rather than looking, we might like the sound of a grandfather clock with its auditory reminders of time.

If we have only a few challenges, we'll get by just fine. However, learning can be negatively impacted when we have a lot of holes in our foundation. In order for learning to be the best it can be, we need a firm foundation. Think about a round wheel of Parmesan cheese—it's hard and compact. You don't notice weak spots of any kind. Compare the wheel of Parmesan with a Swiss cheese, polka-dotted with huge holes. Some baby Swiss has thin, fragile layers of cheese—something is there, but it isn't solid.

Metaphorically, the holes in a foundation for learning can be like the holes in Swiss cheeses—some areas are firm while others are not. Some are simply fragile. This book will help show how to make a foundation for learning firm, so that it can be the best it can be.

After 35 years of working with children, I've created a tool to help pinpoint areas where foundational skills are weak or missing. I began working on this tool because I often heard teachers or parents say that they knew something wasn't quite right with a child but couldn't put a finger on it. This was especially heartbreaking in areas of the country where an occupational therapist wasn't available to evaluate and consult to help determine what the problem might be.

What kinds of problems did I hear repeated? These are typical descriptions of why a child might be chided at home or school:

- Being overly active, disturbing others

- Not wanting to share playground equipment

- Being a "loner"—not participating in "free-time" activities

- Not wanting to wear a particular texture or not tolerating new clothing

- Being overly sensitive to smells or certain foods

- Demonstrating "picky" eating habits

- Consistently picking at insect bites or scabs until they bleed

- Holding one's ears and screaming when going into large rooms, (i.e., the school gym where sound reverberates).

- Having sleep disturbances, including wanting to sleep in their parent's bed.

I began to work on a diagnostic tool that can assist us in identifying and describing each child's particular challenge. After many years of work with hundreds of children, I've created the Foundational Skills Inventory. (See Figure 4: Foundational Skills in a Nutshell and refer to Foundational Skills Inventory found on the inside back cover of book.) By the time you've finished reading this book, the Inventory will make sense and you can use it to discover important information about your child or yourself. Here's an overview of what it covers:

- The first level of the Foundational Skills Inventory evaluates the ability to take in and detect the fact that information is available.

- The second level has to do with the ability to use sensory information and information that comes into the system from muscle/joint sense (*sensory motor processing*).

Figure 4: **Foundational Skills in a Nutshell**

7
- Accomplishment of Complex Tasks with Appropriate Behavior
- Accomplishment of Complex Tasks with "People" Skills

6
- Skills for Tasks

5
- Social Skills

4
- Skills Needed to Help with Higher Learning

3
- Ability to Organize and Process Information

2
- Ability to Use Information from the Senses

1
- Ability to Take in Information
- Ability to Detect Information

- The third level includes being able to organize and process information (*sensory integration*) in order to be able to concentrate and use the capacity for reasoning.

- The fourth level deals with skills needed to help with higher learning.

- The fifth level looks at social skills.

- The sixth level evaluates skills for tasks.

- The seventh level addresses the ability to use complex tasks with appropriate behavior and to accomplish tasks with "people" skills.

Later in this book, the Inventory is further explained, but if you keep this information at the back of your mind as you read further, it will help you to see the "big picture".

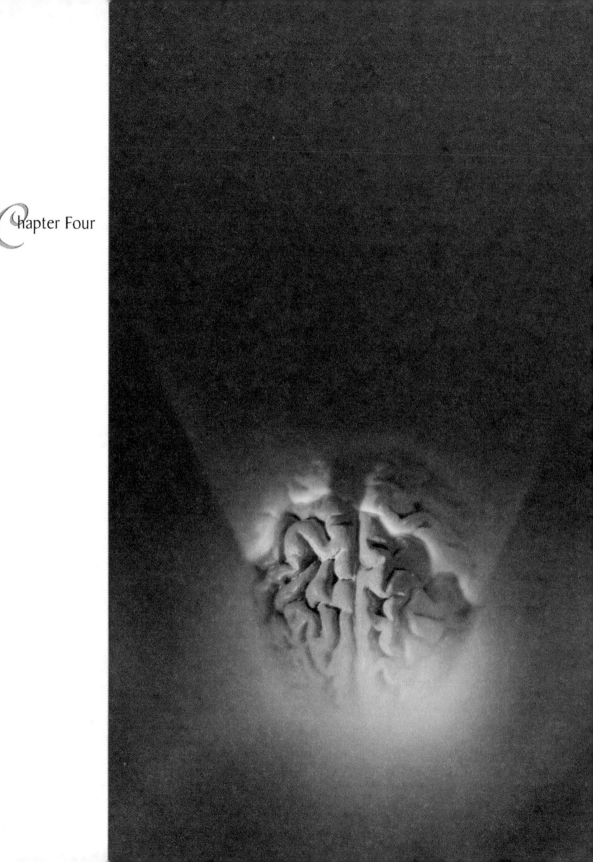

Chapter Four

oving to Learn
A Great Secret Unveiled!

The systems discussed in this chapter sound simple on the surface, but in reality are based in complex neurology. I'll use everyday language—along with some technical terms—to help you become more familiar with the depth of what we're about to explore. We'll skim the surface here, but many books go into great detail about the neuroanatomy involved in our discussion. (Several are included in the bibliography at the end of the book.)

In her book *Smart Moves: Why Learning Is Not All In Your Head*, Carla Hannaford, Ph.D., neurophysiologist and educator explains, "The more closely we consider the elaborate interplay of brain and body, the more clearly one compelling theme emerges: movement is essential to learning....Movement within the womb gives us our first sense of the world and the beginning knowledge and experience of the laws of gravity....Every movement is a sensory-motor event, linked to the intimate understanding of our physical world. . ."[2]

Movement is fundamental and necessary for foundational skills development. What appears to be "child's play" is actually teaching foundational skills. If a child is deprived of adequate, simple play, she may develop behavior that looks as if it is a learning challenge.

Children who learn differently are now being identified. Many of them are constantly moving. Sometimes children are readily labeled hyperactive and given medications to calm them down.

However, as we shall see in this chapter, there can be reasons other than hyperactivity that increase a child's desire to move so much.

Some children seek a continuous barrage of additional stimulation. These children can actually crave movement, might seem to be "on the move" all the time—usually without getting tired—and might even attempt activities that are risky. Many times these children fidget and disturb others around them in the classroom.

Think about the child who uses the playground swing tirelessly, reluctantly sharing the equipment or quitting when recess is over. Now think about the youngster who is on the dance floor for every dance at a wedding, constantly twirling, clapping, and jumping, allowing everyone watching to feel the boundless energy. Yet he never gets tired, or dizzy, or loses balance.

In these scenarios, children crave increased intensity of stimulation in any situation in order to "feel" what is going on. Such children may have a high tolerance for pain and temperature variations—not noticing extreme cold or heat. In many cases, these children run faster, hit harder, kick with more force—and may not want to wear sufficient outdoor clothing when the temperature is low.

The parent or teacher, however, knows that pain is a vital signal. When pain is not present, physical damage can occur. You may need to work with the child to help her recognize that she needs to become aware of the weather and to dress appropriately for the planned activity.

Many parents tell me that these children do not like to wear shoes or socks inside the house. Once they take off their shoes to feel the texture of the universe, it will take a great deal of effort to get those shoes back on!

Increased activity level may also be a disturbance in the system involving touch (*somatosensory/tactile*) in which the system is activated, energized, and on high alert. To this system light touch warns of danger. It can elicit an approach—or avoidance behavior—depending upon the situation. Light touch that is alerting can include:

- A gentle touch on the arm to get the child's attention

- Air from a heating system lightly blowing on the skin

- A light kiss

- Brushing against a stranger in a school hallway

- Wearing new or rumpled clothing that touches the skin unevenly

- Having to take off shoes and socks when feet are sensitive to textures

On the other hand, some children who are sensitive to stimulation might not seek out appropriate activities to help develop a firm foundation. Such children might react in one or more of these ways:

- Avoid excessive movement

- Become anxious when faced with using playground equipment

- Appear uncoordinated in their movements

- Scream, rant, and rave when introduced to situations that involve touching or eating certain textures

- Avoid situations involving undesired sensory input (This is often puzzling to parents and teachers because most children love to play in water, blow bubbles, squish through mud, finger-paint, use sticky glue, pound clay, and squeeze dough for cookies.)

Why are some children involved in lots of squirming in school, talking out of turn, fidgeting, tipping their chairs back on two legs, and being the class clown? In the past, an assumption might have been, "He's just like his father" or "She has an emotional problem."

It's becoming apparent that some of the behavior we see is based on a sensory foundation that isn't mature. It's necessary to look at each person individually to begin to understand what is happening with foundational skills. The best place to start is to look at the activities that might be missing in daily life experiences involving movement, joint interaction, and touch.

In years gone by, children did a great deal of moving in self-directed games after school and on weekends. What happened to simple outside activities that involved running, moving, and increased joint sense awareness? (Many of the old-fashioned games combined the "feel" of gravity with quick thinking, incorporating several of the foundational skills.) Are children in the twenty-first century still playing board and card games, doing crafts, and participating in activities involving cooking from scratch and increasing muscle strength by using the small finger muscles? (You may want to review the excellent book *Electric Bread: A Bread Machine Activity Book for Kids* that is listed in the bibliography. It contains a special section on bread as art.)

Learning to move the body through space and discriminating touch sensations have been hampered by overuse of stationary activities. We've even created the term "couch potato" to describe the child (or adult) constantly sitting at a screen—TV, computer, or video game. In many American homes technology is plentiful, life is convenient, and we're saving time with fast everything.

But we are literally "losing touch." Instead of kneading bread dough beneath their fingers, our children are feeling only the cool smoothness of a computer mouse. Instead of feeling the solid thump of a soccer ball off their feet, our children are feeling only the leg of a chair against their shoes.

In people constantly on the move, foundational skills based in movement and joint interaction (the *vestibular* and *proprioceptive systems*), along with those based in touch and the feeling of being unthreatened (*somatosensory system*) may be immature. Look back at Figure 3: Key to Understanding, to get a picture of how basic movement and touch relate to the foundation of any system.

Before the widespread influences of modern technology—when the basic systems matured within the framework of society—most systems were nourished and satisfied. Now many children have challenges, which include:

- Inability to use their eyes and hands together in a coordinated effort (*eye-hand coordination*)

- Poor balance

- Low muscle tone (*hypotonic muscles*)

- Poor understanding of relationships to objects in space (*visual-spatial relationships*)

- Poor understanding of what is being said to them (*auditory language processing*, at a base level)

- Greater chance of getting upset at seemingly small changes in their environment (*increased emotionality*)

The systems that propel children to move help them to learn by exploring and organizing their world. Both sides of the body learn to work together as they're moving. As the child begins to cross the mid-line of the body—the imaginary line dividing left and right sides of the body—both sides of the brain learn how to communicate more effectively.

If foundational systems are not mature, some children want to move their bodies constantly, in both appropriate and inappropriate situations. (Other children may reflect extroversion rather than immaturity.) When we attempt to stress higher thinking skills and computer skills at an earlier and earlier age, independent exploration, movement, and organization of sensory information may not be sufficiently promoted.

Trying to focus on the task at hand, these academically pushed children may express their cravings for muscle and joint action in a variety of ways. For example, a student who is constantly asking to get a drink of water or is waving his hand to answer a question even before the teacher asks it, in reality may be seeking joint movement to help himself focus. It's up to the adult in charge to recognize that this annoying behavior could actually be indicating sensory needs longing to be satisfied.

We need to give children opportunities to make the most of the information being presented in school. So it behooves us to make sure that subjects such as physical education, marching band, orchestra, music, swimming or other sports programs, and recess are not omitted, but rather are understood for both the primary and secondary functions they provide to the child and to the overall program. (Shooting [basketball] hoops is an excellent activity. Arrange height of hoop to make success challenging but possible.)

When a hard-core academic—such as math or science—follows recess, the nervous system is more readily able to tackle the subject matter. When two academic subjects—such as reading and writing—or two subjects that allow for greater movement—such as gym and music—are scheduled back to back, a great opportunity for enhanced learning is lost. Capitalize on this concept!

Here is what I consider the biggest sensory secret that you can put to work at home and in the classroom: Alternate moving and thinking time. You may be amazed at the results of something as simple as rearranging the order of classes or doing homework after a short "movement activity" time. You may be able to take this concept one step further and include both moving and thinking into one activity. For example, some children do better with reading when they hold the book with two hands and pace. I've seen it work!

The vestibular system is centered in the inner ear. Three occupational therapists—Anne G. Fisher, Elizabeth A. Murray, and Anita C. Bundy—explain its role: "The vestibular system traditionally is viewed as having a role in three major functions: subjective awareness of body position and movement in space; postural tone and equilibrium; and stabilization of the eyes in space during head movements....receptors are the hair cells (cristae) located within the semicircular canals, the utricle, and the saccule of the vestibular labyrinth. . .[the] three semicircular canals. . .[are] oriented at right angles to each other so that they represent all three planes in space....The utricle is a linear accelerometer that detects linear head movement and head tilt...."[3]

Movement can be categorized within planes of action and can be accomplished in a variety of directions. These planes correspond to the planes of the semicircular canals (*angular movement*) and utricle and saccule (*linear movement* and *gravity*) in the inner ear. (See Figure 2: Anatomy of the Inner Ear.)

When the head moves through space, fluid in the ears stimulates the receptors. The planes include:

- Side to side (e.g. dancing)

- Forward and backward (e.g. rocking horse)

- Round and round (e.g. twirling in a tire swing)

- In an orbit (e.g. spinning while going around in an orbit, as seen on an amusement park ride such as the teacup)

- Fast forward in a straight line (e.g. riding in a car or on a bicycle)

- Vibration (e.g. riding in the back of a bus or airplane or driving a wheeled vehicle on rough terrain)

In order to understand and use space concepts (up, down, in, out, behind, beside, by, near, off, over, past, through, throughout, etc.), we have to understand both the words and the meaning they convey to our bodies. These concepts and meanings are learned when the body moves through space with muscles and joints interacting to give the brain information as to where it is in space.

A child needs to understand spatial concepts in order to be able to translate information into the two-dimensional world of paper and pencil—a real part of academics—no mater what grade level is involved. For example, I've seen children who don't fully understand spatial concepts in relationship to their own bodies. So when the teacher gives a specific instruction such as, "Put your name underneath the heading at the top of the page," they have to use higher thinking skills to concentrate on exactly what the teacher means.

These children are having difficulty concentrating on positional information that the teacher mistakenly thinks can be automatically understood by the entire class. Not so. These children get so caught up in interpreting the teacher's first instruction that they lose track of subsequent directives.

Now I have to share one of the saddest secrets that I've observed in dozens of classrooms. **Many children are blamed for not "listening," when in fact they're doing the best that they can. The problem is that the automatic functions—based in the foundational skills—are not kicking in, requiring them to use higher thinking skills to get the job done.** This makes learning tedious, labored, and disagreeable for the child, while even the most positive and motivated educator can become discouraged and even irritated with the process.

Once you grasp the importance of movement and the planes of action, you can find—or create!—a variety of games and activities to help your child mature. A child might do one activity over and over (such as rocking in his chair, lunging, darting, or twirling) because that is the only way that she knows to "feel better." That child needs to learn how to derive pleasure from other movement strategies. When behavior is used to help determine the message in unspoken communication, we can accomplish much. The book *Brain Gym,* by Paul E. Dennison, Ph.D. and Gail E. Dennison, is an excellent reference for a variety of activities for whole-brain learning.

The vestibular/movement system needs input throughout life. It is not as simple as saying "OK, that's done," and checking it off our lifelong list of things to do. But here's some interesting news: this can be the reason that some of us crave the extracurricular activities and have the hobbies that we do!

For example, one of the reasons an airline pilot might feel the need to play racquetball instead of going straight home after a cross-country flight can be explained by the body's need for movement and joint action. The pilot is seeking fast-forward movement, joint/muscle action, and constant changing focus in a fast game of racquetball. This activity provides the system with very different input from the seated-in-one-spot, stressed, focused, highly responsible experience he felt on the job. With this explanation, his family is better able to understand why he is in a much improved mood when he goes to the gym instead of right home after work.

The idea of knowing where you are in space and your relationship to gravity can't be underestimated. When you wake up in the middle of the night to go to the bathroom, the last thing that you want to do is to turn on a bright light. How do you manage to get where you want to be without using your eyes? You do it with your joint/muscle sense. You have *proprioceptors* in all of your joints that give your brain "feed-in/input" as to where you are in space.

This is extremely important in the foundation of learning. Some children (and adults for that matter) have difficulty computing where they are in space. This can be equated with a feeling of being somewhere-out-there with a need to constantly touch someone or something to get a perspective of how the body relates to the space that it is in. I have seen this behavior resemble obsessive/compulsive behavior.

Close your eyes and imagine floating in space. For a while it might feel good, but after a time you want to get back to feeling attached to something. People with a need for additional proprioceptive input might like these things:

- Walking next to walls or gently touching the wall

- Sitting in corners

- Wearing heavy denim or snug, stretchy clothing; wearcing hats

- Using equipment that is "tight" (like driving a sports car or operating a bulldozer)

- Accomplishing activities with "heavy" weight connected with it, or using extra "oomph" in much that they do—to get additional sensory input (Landscaping work or operating a hydraulic drill are choices for some.)

Another child may have difficulty with *postural/gravitational insecurity*. His reaction may look like he's refusing to follow directives for activities in which he has to leave the ground. This child will usually have a difficult time attempting activities that involve anti-gravity situations, such as:

- Going up the ladder of a playground slide

- Sitting on a high stool

- Climbing a rope ladder

- Jumping off a stationary platform

When an attempt is made to force such a child into these situations, she'll pull at anything within reach and usually cry or scream. This type of challenge feels like danger to the system of the child. Too often such behavior is misinterpreted as strong-willed or stubborn instead of an indication that professional assistance is needed. An occupational and/or physical therapist with a background in sensory motor processing/sensory integration can often initiate therapeutic intervention that can make all the difference in the world for this child.

Four-and-a-half-year-old Deanna would scream when she was placed on a kiddy chair 15 inches off the ground. The chair had slits in the back, and she would turn her body and hold on for dear life and scream at the top of her lungs. When I first met her, the classroom teacher was attempting a behavior modification program to motivate Deanna to stop screaming and put together a six-piece, single inset puzzle. Occasionally she would quickly turn around and snatch a piece of candy on the table, throw the puzzle piece into place, turn around, grab hold of the chair and continue to scream.

I observed that Deanna was *gravitationally* and *posturally insecure*. Once she was taken out of the elevated chair and placed on her stomach to work the puzzle, she was able to do the work quietly and efficiently. Deanna's "academics" were transferred from the desk. She would either sit in a corner with a cardboard box as a "desk" (with a cutout for her legs) or lie on her tummy over a bolster. Her meals were moved from the high chair (where she wouldn't eat and would only throw her food and scream) to sitting on a plastic tablecloth on the floor. (Her parents had already resorted to her eating on the floor but felt terrible about it and would tell no one.)

In the course of a year of occupational therapy, Deanna was able to participate in activities that included using the swings and slide on the playground. Eventually she became a happy child who could accomplish activities close to her developmental level. As she became a joy-filled child, so did everyone around her!

"Physiology"—the way in which you position yourself—tells your body on an unconscious level how you're feeling by creating the internal status that is necessary to feel in that particular way. The best thing you can do for yourself when you are "down" is to create the physiology of being in a good mood:

- Hold your head up high, shoulders straight, chin up, put a smile on your face

- Walk briskly, arms swinging by your side

- Breathe deeply

- Listen to uplifting music

If you try these simple things, your body will think you're in a good mood even if your brain wants to talk you out of it! This is one of the best moves you can make when you want to reduce stress and are on a tight schedule.

Remember, emotion follows motion. When you need additional motivation to accomplish a task, put yourself in the movement pattern that is needed to begin the task, and that will begin the flow. You may be surprised with the results!

Children need to be engaged in a variety of activities, not only sitting at terminals and/or reading all day. At seminars and workshops I lead, educators and parents frequently request a list of activities that make up a good "sensory diet." (I like to compare a good sensory diet to making sure we're feeding our families a balanced, nutritious diet that includes all the basic food groups.)

If this discussion makes sense to you—and if you have a family with minimal deficiencies—you can devise a sensory diet yourself, constructing a program with suggestions from a number of activity books. Carol Stock Kranowitz, a preschool teacher and author of the book *The Out-of-Sync Child: Recognizing and Coping with Sensory Integration Dysfunction*, provides several chapters of activities for children. More recently she has written *The Out-of Sync Child Has Fun: Activities for Kids with Sensory Integration Dysfunction*, which is an excellent reference. Many of my own suggestions are outlined in the chapter "Creating a Sound Sensory Diet" later in this book.

The real beauty of enhancing foundational skills is that the process can be both enjoyable and educational. Set a realistic goal for yourself and enjoy planning activities that are not only fun for your family, but will help your child throughout life as well.

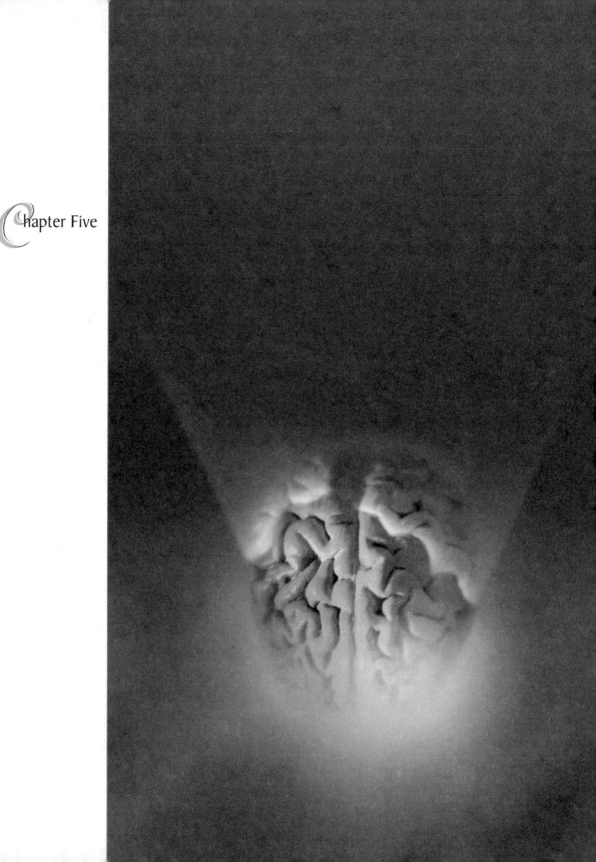

Chapter Five

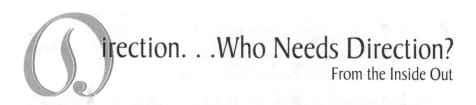

Direction. . .Who Needs Direction?
From the Inside Out

Do you know an otherwise neurotypical adult who has trouble identifying his left from his right hand or has difficulty reading maps and following geographic directions? Such a person may be extremely bright—but unable to find his way around the shopping mall. This is not an uncommon problem.

Knowledge of left and right sides of the body is called *laterality*. Understanding directions outside of the body is known as directionality. (Understanding the concept of laterality usually takes place before learning *directionality*.) Most people assume that directionality happens automatically, but that isn't always so. The roots for this ability are found on the first levels of foundational skills. (Refer to the Foundational Skills Inventory found on the inside back cover of this book.)

Directionality is required to understand many games, oral or written directions, and maps. A person learns critically important information from movement felt in the muscles, moving and touch, position in space, relationship to gravity, and from using both sides of the body.

Bilateral-motor coordination is the ability to use both sides of the body together. It is also represented at an early stage on the Foundational Skills Inventory. Watch infants playing patty-cake, clapping, or banging two blocks together and you see the basis for bilateral-motor coordination. During these activities, the brain is filtering information, reflexes are maturing, the child is learning where she is in space through the use of prepositional space concepts, as well as learning where her body parts are located (*body concept*), and how she feels about herself (*body image*).

Motor planning is developing as we get an idea, structure and sequence the steps that are needed to accomplish the task, and then follow through with the activity. Large muscles are coordinating with fine muscles of the hands and fingers. Other learning is also taking place—focusing and directing attention, and adjusting posture to participate in the task. With efficient sensory integration, organizing and processing a wealth of information is occurring. This process requires mature sensory systems. People with immature sensory systems face challenges in organizing and processing information.

Often an infant can be seen to have a right- or left-hand preference. The preferred hand is used for thumb sucking or reaching for toys. When the child begins to accomplish more sophisticated fine motor behaviors, such as coloring and cutting, a *hand dominance* (*working hand*) emerges. (The opposite hand becomes the assisting or *helping hand*.)

Whether a child is right- or left-handed is not an issue in foundational learning. Once hand dominance is established and the dominant hand is able to cross over to the other side of the body—a process called *crossing the midline*—better communication develops between the right and left hemispheres of the brain. This is called *lateralization of cerebral function* and is instrumental in allowing the brain to function at an optimal level.

Mixed dominance can be seen in individuals who perform some tasks well with one hand and others with the opposite hand. (This should not be confused with *ambidexterity*, in which tasks are

performed equally well with either hand.) During the learning process, a left- or right-handed child may have a new skill demonstrated
by a person who has the opposite hand dominance. For example,
a left-handed mom who teaches a right-handed preschooler to cut
might demonstrate the technique using her left hand. Thus her right-
handed child might learn to cut with her left hand because that was
the way it was taught.

Why are people having such a hard time with endurance
for the work at hand? I suggest that our children are not developing the small (*intrinsic*) muscles of the hands as was done in the
past. Where are the games played repeatedly—checkers, marbles,
jacks, dominoes, Sorry, and Monopoly? We held cards in our hands
and shuffled while we were mentally working out our next play.
What happened to jigsaw puzzles that stayed on a special table for
us to work on whenever we had a few minutes of leisure? When I
was growing up we engaged in these activities on a daily basis! We
didn't realize we were learning basic life skills—we were simply
enjoying games and puzzles as a normal part of our lives.

Remember the crafts that required using our fingers with
strength and endurance? Making leather projects involved pressing
hard with cutting tools and then lacing pieces together. We learned
paper crafts that required using a punch, stapler, and crayons. How
about all of that tactile information gathered from our fingers when
using finger-paint, glue, papier-mâché, and old-fashioned, hard-to-
manage clay?

What about cooking projects such as pizza and bread dough
where we kneaded until our fingers ached? Or making cookies from
scratch—combining ingredients, stirring stiff dough, using the rolling pin and a lot of pressure?

In this age of technology, games and crafts do not get much needed emphasis in the classroom or on the playground! Out of school, these ideas are considered rainy-day activities during vacations. Crafts are often reserved for young children, since it isn't "cool" for older children to do such projects. Besides that, many of them are busy sitting in front of an electronic screen.

Regardless of what's in vogue, the child's developing system needs to squeeze, twist, pull, push, and poke—and our children aren't doing it enough! The importance of how our hand muscles need to strengthen is not widely understood. How much energy does it take to move a computer mouse around? Not much—and some of our children have "mushy" hands to prove it.

Let's talk about handwriting, another of my favorite topics. I believe several things have led to poor handwriting:

- Natural, everyday hand-strengthening activities are easily overlooked.

- Children often do not learn the correct way to hold a pencil and therefore develop an inefficient grasp pattern (See figure 5, page 59).

- Teachers don't have time to emphasize handwriting and/or there is limited opportunity to practice handwriting on a daily basis.

The "third-finger grasp" (*adaptive tripod grasp*, see figure 6 on page 60) can be used with some people who have a hard time using the traditional mature hand-grasp pattern (See figure 7, page 60). In this grasp, the pencil is held between the index and third finger instead of the web of the thumb. Try using this pattern with your "assisting" hand to see what kind of a signature you can create. Now do the same thing using the traditional pattern. Which one works best?

The thumb wrap (below) is an inefficient pattern that is often seen today. It uses the wrist rather than the fingers to direct the writing instrument.

So, who needs direction? We all do! Yet it's an overlooked foundational skill. Let's shuffle the Uno cards at a revived Family Game Night, stretch elastic pizza dough with our kids, and allow much-needed time for supervised practice of handwriting at home and school. All in favor of my proposed revival, raise your dominant hand!

Figure 5 **Thumb Wrap Grasp: an inefficient pattern that is often used today**

Figure 6 **Adaptive Tripod Grasp: an efficient pattern that can be used**

Figure 7 **Tripod Grasp: traditional "typo" efficient mature grasp pattern**

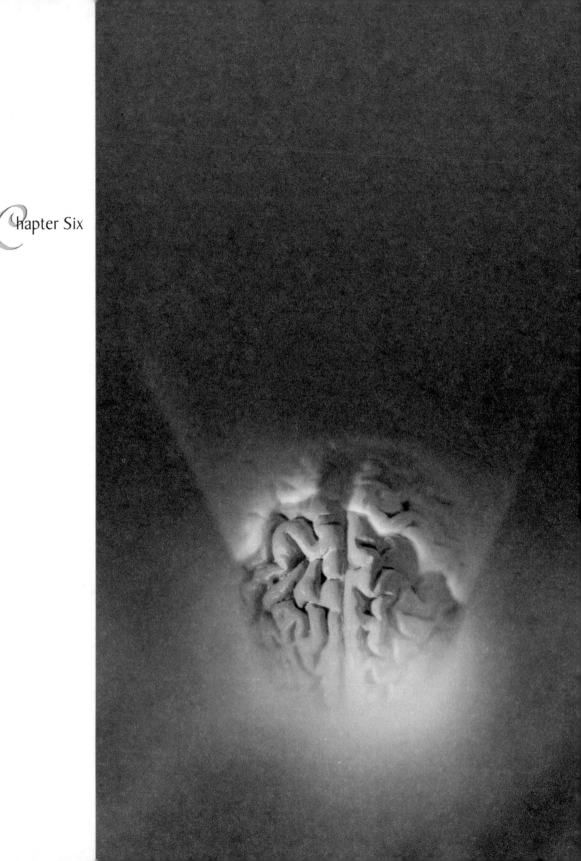

Chapter Six

The Power of Touch
Energy from the Heart

The significance of touch to human development is grossly underestimated.

We need touch. . .
    we lack touch. . .
        we crave touch. . .
           and often we're looking for it in all the wrong places.

We're becoming less sensitive to touch, and many of our children are having challenges because of it. Many of our children know only the numb state of *desensitization*—a lack of feeling.

In the past, babies were often carried in the arms of another human being. Today, children are often carried in plastic containers where they lie on their backs and gaze at either the ceiling (boring, even for an infant), the top of the carrier (same old thing), or on rare and lucky occasions, clouds in the sky. They're seated in tightly confined carriers in the back seat of cars facing a blank "wall." Safety is our primary concern, as it should be. So the challenge becomes, how can we develop secure, safe seating that also encourages the developing sensory systems?

Children are losing out on learning subtle communication skills that could readily be gained when carried in a position where they are eye to eye with another human being—where they are in the middle of the action. The pull of gravity on the child's joints (*proprioception*) and the constant challenge to stay in an upright position gives an infant a workout, even though the person carrying the infant isn't aware of it. Unfortunately, many of today's children are in static positions for long periods of time, with their eyes focused on nothing in particular.

If Jamie is lucky, the seat that is used for the car and stroller will be different, because at least moving from one place to another will offer brief holding time. He might otherwise have to cry, scream, rant, and rage in order to be picked up or have his position changed. What are we teaching our children at such an early age? Could it be "car-seat rage"?

Amanda is taken out of a car seat and then lovingly placed into an all-purpose stroller. She will be in this position for the duration of the outing and then will go back into a car seat. Her parents don't realize that Amanda hasn't had a real change in position for hours!

What about Diana, who fusses but doesn't "make a scene"? Her grandparents are uncertain about the cause of her discomfort. Before offering her a cookie or a bottle, her grandmother can try shifting her position. If that works, the fussy behavior might be communicating just that—a need to move around—and not the need for food. Using food to calm us can lead to lifelong eating patterns that are hard to break!

Placement in a "container" might be convenient, but static seating should be limited. If it is prolonged, children lose out on the benefits of sensory "feed in." Children need to be upright to see what's happening around them. They need opportunities to shift their weight and experience the pull of gravity, while securely maintaining their posture. Children with easy-going personalities can be more peaceful about many hours spent confined and will miss out on the additional stimulation that might have been available had they made more of a fuss.

Fortunately, the old-fashioned infant sling (like Snugli by Even Flow) is regaining popularity. It offers parents who can carry their child a better choice than unbendable plastic carriers. Safety comes first; then introduce a variety of positions for your infant; finally, become aware of the quality of stimulation in the visual field.

With increased awareness of Sudden Infant Death Syndrome, children are positioned on their backs to avoid problems with suffocation. While keeping safety issues in mind, we need to look at positioning options **for times other than sleeping.** Kept on their backs a great deal of the time, some children are developing flattened heads (positional plagio cephaly)—as well as missing out on developmental milestones that are stimulated when they explore positions on their own. Ultimately, when children are positioned on their backs for long periods of waking time, they are learning that the world comes to them with very little effort. They are not "working" with joints and muscles to feel where they are in space to develop a good relationship with gravity.

When you have time to supervise your baby, put him on his stomach. Allow experimentation with positions like pushing up on his forearms with his head bobbing in the air—he's learning to deal with gravity. Let him rock his body in preparation for creeping, and gently fall sideways—he's feeling the pull of gravity. The curiosity that leads to crawling, creeping and exploring independently should not be delayed or stifled. Time for exploring and organizing sensory information has to be diligently supervised. Often this type of time is at a premium in day care and nursery schools.

Children need to have time where they learn to push up on their arms, hands, legs, and feet. They need to be safely on the floor, grass, or carpet—where they're exposed to a variety of textures—crawling, creeping, safely touching, exploring, organizing, and integrating the information that's coming to them. Children need to do this over and over, day after day with people who have a vested interest in them, and with whom they will develop meaningful relationships. They need adults who want to stimulate and be with them, hold and touch them, and who take pleasure in seeing the miracle of what is happening before their eyes.

Too often in group situations—such as day care—children are either in a "resting" mode, where they are on their backs, or in a "doing" mode, where they're seated. They are not usually left on their stomachs because this is the "get-up-and-go" position that requires supervision for safety and is not desirable when a few caregivers are trying to contain a large number of children.

Now let's get to the core issue with touch. The tactile/touch system (*somatosensory system*) is a foundational system that has a two-fold process: protection and discrimination.

The protective system is highly active at birth, yet it is something we don't even think about. Light touch alerts to danger. Try a small experiment right now. Lightly move your hand over the hair on your opposite arm; doing this is usually uncomfortable.

When danger is sensed, the protective system goes into high gear. You might experience this when someone moves into your "personal space," is following you, or stares at you for a prolonged time. A feeling of "fight or flight" can take over.

When an infant feels threatened, we often hear about it, loud and clear! In the case of a child who is on "automatic protection," a lot of energy has to be dedicated to consciously controlling behavior. Too much energy may have to be invested in what shouldn't be a concern at all!

As a child matures, the protective system remains available, but is less often in the "alert" mode. A little-known sensory secret is that, in some children, this system can be overly active when it shouldn't be! This can look like high activity level for no apparent reason. This can be misjudged as a behavior problem, when in reality the protective system is overactive and getting in the way.

Using light touch alerts the protective system and can make the problem worse! That helps explain why activities involving light touch are so objectionable to some children. For them, the feeling of new clothing is intolerable because sizing allows the material to touch the skin at various "pin" points. Luke told me that it felt like little needles pricking his skin all over his body. His mom wanted to know why she had to wash every new outfit ten times before he'd wear it. An insect bite can drive another person wild. Annie would scratch every bite until her clothing was dotted with blood.

For other children, finger-painting is out of the question, and using sticky substances such as glue, paste, or wet papier-mâché elicits tantrums like no others! What do all of these activities have in common? They all provide light touch. They alert the overly active protective system—to danger.

Ron frequently ended up in the principal's office because of striking out at fellow students. After pondering why this happened—as he had done countless times before—the principal lightly placed her hands on his shoulders and agreed with him that this behavior would not happen again. Ron looked at her as if he were trying to keep himself from striking her! This was puzzling to the principal, since Ron had demonstrated such sincere resolve not to do it again. After our discussion on the protective system, she realized that Ron had an over-reactive protective system, and that it did indeed take a lot of energy to keep from striking out at her, too!

Ron's system perceived people in the space around him as threatening, and he would automatically do whatever it took to get rid of the danger. (This was not something he thought about; it was an automatic response.) Even the light touch of the principal's hands on his shoulders brought about the same reaction, and it took a lot of thinking/control (use of *cognition*), not to strike out at her. When she substituted "heavy touch/pressure" on his shoulders, his system perceived the action differently, and he didn't overreact.

With a therapeutic program including a regularly scheduled regimen of deep pressure and joint compression, Ron became a "well behaved" boy. Ron's parents and teachers became aware of the need to reduce "light touch" experiences, until his system was normalized. Specific actions included:

- Having Ron stand at the beginning or end of the line, because when he stood in the middle, other children could rub against him lightly

- Moving his desk away from the direct line of the air ventilating system in math class

- Moving his desk from the middle of the room in science class, where more children would naturally raise air currents as they walked by

Ron also needed to engage in activities that gave his muscles and joints additional touch pressure, such as:

- Helping to move the desks and vacuum the room after art class

- Playing soccer and other vigorous games

- Running active errands, such as taking books to the office and carrying groceries in from the car

- Engaging in water play in the pool

- Playing the piano and bongo drums

- Sleeping in a cocoon of tight-fitting sheets at night

Fortunately, this story had a positive ending. Over time Ron became a happy child who was no longer a frequent visitor in the principal's office. Without understanding the protective system it could have been a very different story, indeed!

Helping the protective system to adjust can be accomplished through the use of "heavy touch and/or heavy work patterns," such as joint/muscle action with some weight that helps the tactile system to feel where it is in space and/or where the edges of the body are. Some of us like wearing clothes that are naturally heavy—such as fur coats, jeans, beaded jackets—or that fit tightly to the skin—such as spandex tights, bathing caps, and head bands. Infants sometimes calm when swaddled snugly in a blanket.

Some adults like to drive vehicles that require more joint pressure to operate them, such as sports cars, trucks, or SUVs with stick shift. Others prefer massage therapists who use heavy-handed movements. By looking at your own preferences, you may discover patterns you use to help your own system feel better.

Three-year-old Joey loved to help his dad with morning chores on the farm where they owned and cared for huge draft horses.

He delighted in filling his child's-sized wheelbarrow with manure and pushing it out to the pile outside the barn. Huffing and puffing with endearing little grunts, Joey engaged in functional heavy-work patterns. His mother noticed that he took a good nap and was much more pleasant on the days that he "helped" his father. She used to think it was because of the nap—but now she realizes that the joint interaction of loading and pushing the wheelbarrow not only tired him out but also helped him to create a firm foundation for learning.

It is interesting to note that *peripheral* (side) vision alerts the protective system. This is the vision that is usually checked when we get our driver's license and we are asked to look at a stationary point while we identify an object as it comes into our side line of vision. This vision is more primitive than the vision required when our hands and eyes work together (*focal vision*).

Have you seen a child flick his fingers on the side of his head? Have you seen a child look at you while his head was pointing forward and his eyes turned to the side? Visual children may be using peripheral vision instead of focal vision. In the past, we would use behavior modification with a reinforcer (*usually food*) to get such a child to "look at me." Now we know that another method that engages the protective system might be more effective.

Here is my favorite sensory secret, a wonderful intervention to help focus attention to the task at hand at an automatic level of thinking. **Create tasks that engage both hands in accomplishing the desired activity *(bilateral activity)*. When both hands are engaged in activity, the protective system lays the groundwork to pay attention in order to avoid danger!**

In order to obtain better focal vision (vision for eye and hand coordination), plan activities that involve using both hands, such as:

- Rolling cookie dough or clay

- Folding or cutting paper

- Throwing large balls or stacking large blocks

- Building sand castles

- Playing in the water and learning to swim

- Dressing large dolls or stuffed animals

- Clapping or beating time to music

- Singing motion songs, such as "Itsy-Bitsy Spider"

- Playing instruments such as the tambourine, rhythm sticks, sand blocks, bongo drums, keyboard, or cymbals

- Holding a paper or book with both hands while reading

- Stringing beads and completing lacing projects (Do not use this activity for children who place inedible objects in mouth)

- Using interlocking toys like pop beads and barrels that can be pulled apart and pushed together

Recently I talked to Toni, a woman in a workplace with lighted candles positioned at shoulder- and eye-level. This made her uncomfortable, but she didn't know why since she ordinarily liked candles. She knew that she couldn't work efficiently with them lit—and that her boss wasn't happy about her going around and blowing them out!

When we discussed the possibility that the candles were at a level of her peripheral vision and were alerting her protective system to subtle danger, a whole arena for negotiation was opened. All that Toni had to do to solve her problem was to move the candles to a safe position outside the area of her peripheral vision. Sometimes knowing about our sensory needs can improve our lives with very little effort!

The protective system also deals with our relationship to gravity. When Andrew is not secure in his ability to leave Mother Earth, he has difficulty using equipment that places him above the ground (such as the slide, monkey bars, rope ladder, balance beam, rocking horse, etc.)

The *discriminating tactile system* includes the ability to identify textures (hard, soft, rough, wet, smooth, sticky, cold, warm, etc.), the ability to discriminate touch on the skin (*surface pressure* or a *point of pressure*), and identification of size and shape. We know this system well—it helps us to feel the differences in textures. We learn about it at an early age.

But what we don't learn as infants is that it also includes the sophisticated ability to identify objects using touch without vision (*stereognosis*). This includes your ability to get into your change cup and take out the correct coins to pay the toll, while still driving with both eyes on the road. It is demonstrated in a child's glee while using the "feelie box" at school. It also includes the ability to discriminate touch in such a fine manner that you can identify shapes and letters that are drawn on the skin without looking (*graphesthe-*

sia). If for just one day you had to function with gloves or mittens

on, you'd have some idea how it feels to have a challenge in the ability to use discriminating tactile awareness.

Today, there is a heightened awareness and sensitivity to physical touch. Educators have to be mindful of how a congratulatory pat on the back could be misconstrued. A child who innocently kisses another child can have problems beyond the wildest dreams of our ancestors. However, while caution is important in our litigious world, we also need to realize that touch is a sensory need, especially for the infant and young child.

I've heard this advice for new parents—*always* pick up a crying infant because it's simply not possible to "spoil" a child in the first year of life. While I might agree that it's not possible to spoil an infant, with a good sensory diet in place, it may not always be necessary to pick up a child every time she cries. Let me explain exactly what I mean.

A child who is getting sufficient touching and bonding may not need to be picked up if he begins crying in the middle of the night. He might fall back asleep after Dad rubs his back with a gentle rocking motion and talks to him softly for a few moments. Patting and talking is **loving**, it is **familiar**, and it **carries a deep message in a short time**. But if familiar, loving touch and the sound of a nurturing voice is rarely experienced, the child might need a greater amount of sensory input to calm down—he may indeed need to be picked up and held for a few minutes.

As they grow up, many young people are looking for touch in all the wrong places. They're moving towards sexual activity at earlier and earlier ages. A growing number of teen-aged girls are expressing the desire to have and care for a baby. Often they don't realize the long-term implications and responsibilities involved.

If we see this desire for motherhood as a form of communication and hear the cry for love, the message rings loud and clear—"I need to bond with someone; I need to touch someone; I need someone to love, and to have someone love me back. I don't want to be numb anymore. Help me to 'feel' again!" This is the only way the adolescent can manage the "problem" as she sees it, because in her mind it is the only logical solution.

This cry has its basis in wanting to be mothered or nurtured herself. This is not an ignorant, stupid, unreasonable desire—it is a basic need. In the desensitized world in which we live, arguing with and shaming a teen into seeing the inadequacy of her position creates defensiveness. Such a teen should be commended for wanting to feel again! She realizes that something is missing, and she's trying to fill the gap. Granted, as adults we can readily see that having a baby is not a preferable option, but it's important for us to understand why it appears as a solution to the teen.

For some teens, community volunteering can help to fill this void. Such a teen deserves to feel the gratitude and see the appreciation of a mother who needs help teaching her youngsters. While working in a hospital, she can touch and bring a smile to the face of a child who is waiting for cancer surgery. She may see the love in the eyes of a first-grader and hear his proud voice as he reads. She may feel the soft squeeze of her hand by the senior citizen she visits with Meals on Wheels. If she's not getting what she needs from her own family, community involvement can help build self-esteem and allow her to feel again.

On the other hand, some teenagers (frequently boys) may exhibit loud, obnoxious behavior. Too often their parents attempt to deal with them on an intellectual level. The teen is talked to and screamed at. The parents attempt to shame him into improved behavior. Yet nothing seems to work.

Think about it—a teenaged boy who needs intense input to feel **anything** is being asked to give up the very behavior that gives him some stimulation! Public reaction, tears of the parent, and shock of the severity of the situation all feed the teen who is constantly manipulating situations in order to have "feeling" about anything at all!

The person who does not feel in healthy, functional ways will continue to find methods to have some feeling—and will not have qualms about how it is accomplished. Goals and purpose in life are rarely apparent in the life of a desensitized person. Escalating unacceptable behaviors can be predicted, as previously outrageous behaviors become mundane. More violent scenarios are planned and implemented in order to "get a feel for life."

In her book *Parenthood by Proxy—Don't Have Them If You Won't Raise Them*, Dr. Laura Schlessinger states, "Family life with children requires more emphasis on children than Power Bar breakfasts and kissing them off to school or day care, shuttles from after-school day care to extracurricular activities, wolfing down fast-food takeout, unsupervised evening activities, and weekend teen mall roaming. Frankly, children's very existence needs to be the central focus of the family...."[4]

We must learn how to bond with our children and allow them to become compassionate, loving people. In order to do this, we need greater balance in managing the sensory diets of our children from birth on. They need to have a great deal of appropriate touch in their lives and we have to figure out how this can be done in our fast-moving society.

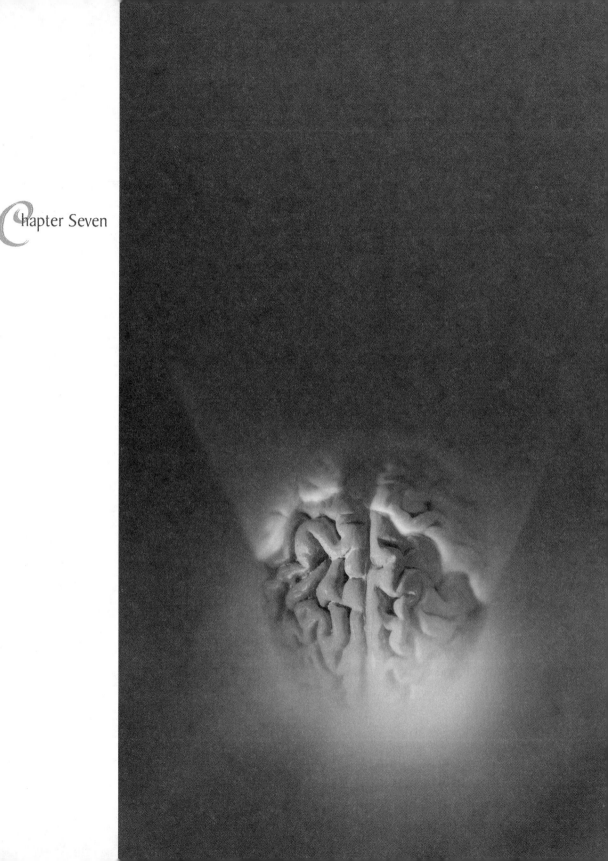

Chapter Seven

What You See and Hear Is What You Get
Sometimes Less Is More!

When we think of our eyes, we usually think about how clearly we see things (called *visual acuity*). We may also consider whether or not we need corrective lenses. Perhaps we contemplate a surgical procedure to correct impaired vision.

This chapter explores an area of vision that is not so familiar. It's called *visual perception,* i.e. the capacity to give meaning to what is seen. We all see things differently, even when we're looking at the same scene!

Have you ever been an eyewitness to an accident? Did you notice that other eyewitnesses recounted a different version of what actually happened? Visual-spatial perception—along with our previous experience, learning style (left/right/whole brain), emotions at the time (psychology), internal body chemistry (physiology), and foundational system maturation (neurology)—all enter into our ability to perceive our world.

Visual perception includes the ability to:

- Discriminate between the same and different aspects of what we see (observing in a parking lot what characteristic makes all the red cars the same and what characteristics make them different)

- Remember what we see and the sequence of events (reading the directions for completing a task and remembering the order in which they are to be accomplished)

- Know that objects retain their constancy (they do not get bigger and smaller as they go near and far away, as it would look to a person waving good-bye as another person walks away. Nor do they change size when they move up and down, as objects look smaller when viewed from atop a high building)

- Filter the important information that we see, and leave irrelevant details behind (finding hidden objects, finding the hidden pictures, putting colorform shapes back onto the original outline of the shape on the cardboard)

- Recognize a part of something before it represents a whole object (visual closure, such as the ability to identify dot-to-dot pictures before they are completed)

- Mentally picture objects in space (*space visualization*) (figuring out which containers will fit leftover food, attempting to fit an oversized piece of luggage in the overhead compartment on a plane, or mentally rearranging furniture before physically moving it)

Here's another important sensory secret. **Sometimes a child can have difficulty with perception because of too much sensory input.**

One example of overload in the area of *visual-figure-ground* perception is a classroom that is filled with murals, charts, pictures, mobiles, posters, bulletin-board displays, lists, and diagrams on all the walls and ceiling. This can be too much visual stimulation. For some children, each item is screaming for attention—but there is too much all at once. For others, of course, this much stimulation is fulfilling.

Many people believe that learning will take place more quickly in an environment with lots of visual stimulation to capture the attention. However, for the child with visual perceptual overload, it can be distracting and difficult to work in such a room. Such a child will gratefully go into a plain study area in order to be able to pay attention to the task at hand.

I've also met adults who don't like a lot of sensory input. Their homes are decorated in a very sparse fashion. They find that if there is too much on the walls they cannot relax—or might even feel dizzy.

People who seek less sensory stimulation are often appreciative when their needs are recognized and they're validated for doing what they feel is best for themselves. Our bodies seek the balance that is needed for our individual selves to be the best we can be. We're now understanding the importance of listening to our own system as it tries to cope with the sensory situations in which we find ourselves.

If a child has a problem accomplishing perceptual tasks, she can have a great deal of difficulty paying attention to what is important in class. It might even be a challenge to reproduce forms and letters (writing the alphabet) even though the motor (muscle) ability to do so might be intact. When there are too many "challenges" in this area, learning can be difficult indeed!

A similar phenomenon is *auditory-figure-ground* perception. This ability allows a person to tune in to important sounds that are happening amid a cacophony—and not be distracted by unimportant sounds.

Some children have difficulty tuning out extraneous sounds—such as an airplane overhead, a train or boat whistle, the howling wind outside the classroom, or even the hum of the fluorescent lights—as they're trying to pay attention to their work. It can be difficult to pay attention to the textbook or the teacher because all the sounds seem of equal importance to their system.

Echoes in large rooms with high ceilings—such as gymnasiums and cafeterias—are sometimes so overwhelming to the system that a child might stand with his hands on his ears screaming or crying. This child might tear off earphones or not allow inserts to be placed in his ears.

Ricky would have a full-blown tantrum every time the family prepared for church. So the family split up and one parent took the rest of the children to church while the other stayed home with the sensitive son. The parents investigated auditory-figure-ground perception and realized that their customary pew—close to the speakers carrying voices and music—was over stimulating to Ricky's system.

Small changes in family habits can make a huge difference. They selected seats farther away from the speakers, allowed Ricky to wear hats that covered his ears, and worked with an occupational therapist on a home program to improve his sensory processing/sensory integration. Paired with new understanding, these simple changes made an enormous difference for the whole family's bonding and enjoying time together!

In the twenty-first century, information is flying past us in multimedia glitz. Our eyes and ears are assaulted by live entertainment, television programs, commercials, movies, dancing e-mail greeting cards, and other interactive activities.

Many teachers must compete with professional entertainment to maintain most children's attention. For the majority of American students this is just "life in the fast lane." However, for children with learning challenges, this constant bombardment of eyes and ears can be dreadful! Trying to keep up with all that is blasting the system at once can be difficult, and sometimes impossible. It can cause anxious behavior and emotional *lability* (tantrums, outbursts, etc.). Sometimes the system simply shuts down.

One mom told me about her infant regularly putting her arm out to stop the automatic swing that her parents used to calm her. This child learned at a very early age how to stop the stimulation!

Unfortunately, many children never figure out how to protect themselves from overload. As parents and teachers, we have a responsibility to make sure our kids are getting enough—but not too much!—sensory stimulation.

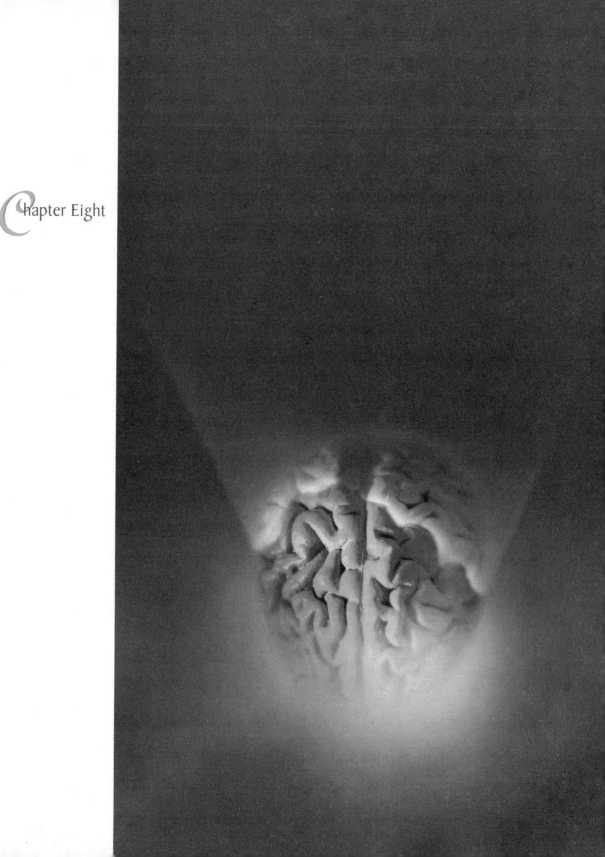

Chapter Eight

Color Your World
There's a Rainbow of Options

Color is an enhancement to our world, yet many times we take it for granted. Color can be a motivator. It adds variety and excitement to areas that could be dull. Close your eyes and imagine an arch in the sky of only black, white, and shades of gray. Now picture a vivid, shimmering rainbow. It's not hard to decide which image is more attractive!

Color has always been an integral part of life and language. This is seen in some of our common expressions, such as "to have the blues," "to be red with rage," "to be in the pink," "to hate it with a purple passion," or "to be green with envy."

Here are some generalizations about color:

- Red is an exciting color that broadcasts energy, alertness, motivation, and power. Restaurants that use the red/orange theme are often fast-food eateries geared to in-and-out business.

- Blue gives a feeling of quiet restfulness. Could it be why the sky is blue?

- Green gives a feeling of harmony and balance. Being in nature can restore that feeling—I wonder if all that green helps?

We're now learning that color is all-important to learning life skills and can actually enhance education. Some children have a special affinity for color. The following are thumbnail sketches from my own therapeutic experience.

- Marie was able to improve her scores when she wrote her spelling words vertically and made each one a different color. She always started with green for "go."

- Jay had difficulty finishing his reading and math. When his favorite light blue transparency was placed over his work, he was able to concentrate on it.

- Color writing (each letter a different color) helped Lori with the direction of her letters.

- Ron remembered the sequence of instruction when he wrote each direction as a separate paragraph, in a different color.

- Connie was able to finish her math with greater accuracy when she was allowed to take a piece of construction paper (color of her choice) and place it under her work-sheet. Her parents found that this technique worked at home as well as it did at school.

These are all relatively simple strategies that can be used or adapted in a variety of situations. Thank goodness for colored marking pens and pencils and construction paper! If one of your children seems to be especially color sensitive, you can experiment with colorful solutions without breaking your budget.

However, for other children, the solutions may require more of an investment in thought, time, and creativity. Consider Kathy's predicament.

To save precious time in the morning, the night before she always picked out the clothes that she would wear to school the next day. But too often her parents were dismayed when she was late for the bus because she was trying on outfit after outfit and complaining that they didn't "feel right."

Once Kathy's sensitivity to color was observed, the family agreed to wake her up a little earlier, and her mother would ask her what color she "felt like" that day. Kathy would then choose clothing that matched her feeling. Not only did she get ready in record time, but she also seemed to do better at school!

Mark was able to calm down after recess by sitting on a large beanbag chair. The weight of the beans on his joints helped to calm him down. His teacher noticed that Mark calmed down faster when he sat on blue or green, rather than on red or orange beanbags!

Sometimes when children can't learn—or when a child doesn't sleep well through the night—a different color scheme can make a dramatic difference. For example, changing from red, orange, or bright fluorescent colors to white, beige, tans, light greens, or blues can improve the situation in the study or sleeping area.

Margaret's bedroom was decorated in red, white, and blue with a Centennial theme. When Margaret's parents changed her sheets from red to white and moved her bed to face the white portion of the wall, Margaret was able to fall asleep sooner.

If cafeteria food fights and too much loud talking in the library are causing chaos in your school, look at the color scheme. Try changing extensive areas that are red, orange, and fluorescent yellow to light blue, green, beige, or white.

I've observed children become energized to do their work by simply placing a piece of red construction paper on their seat or by having them move to a red chair. I've also seen overly active children calm down when sitting on blue or green construction paper or chairs of those colors.

It's interesting to see how something so simple can change a negative work pattern. Take a look at the colors around you—and your children—and learn more about how they affect your behavior at a level that is "below-thinking" (*sub-cortical*).

Christine Page, M.D., a physician and leader in the healing profession, has a wide-ranging interest in all forms of healing, which enables her to play a major role in the widespread use of complementary medicine in the British National Health Service. She teaches internationally, recognizing that the path to well being involves expansion of consciousness, and has been one of the teachers who helped me to understand the importance of color in our lives. Dr. Page writes about the "colour" of emotions in her book *Frontiers of Health, From Healing to Wholeness* (see bibliography).

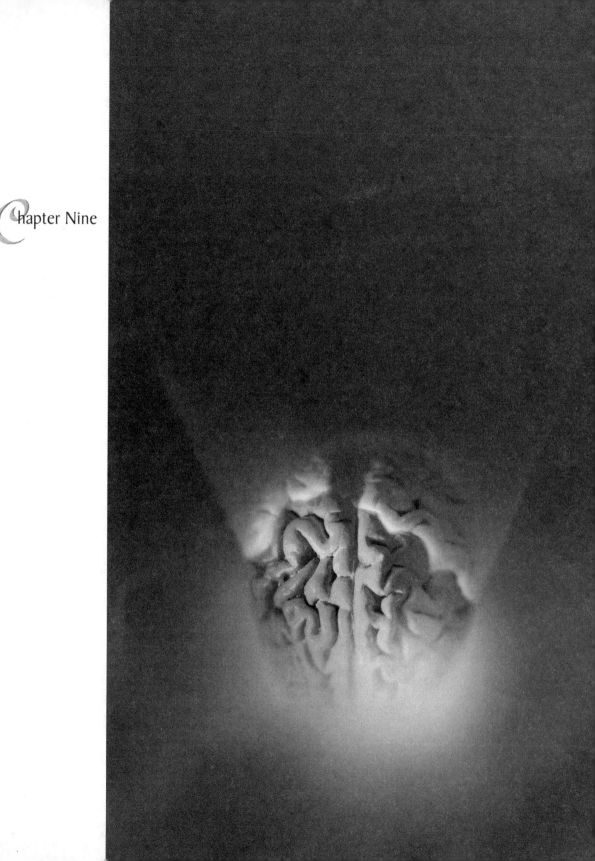

Chapter Nine

The Joy of Eating?
Not Always!

And now we've reached one of my favorite topics. If you like to eat like I like to eat, it would seem as if the whole world should see this activity as one glorious celebration to be cherished! Must I admit that I'm Italian and love to cook and eat? And I also find great satisfaction in helping challenged children learn to enjoy their food, some for the first time.

Why is it that some children do **not** like to eat? Some of them will eat only sour, salty, pungent, tangy foods and others will eat only one texture, say crunchy or soft foods. Some people say that they don't like smooth textures with crunchy in the same bite, and some people can't stand soft, mushy consistencies. Why? Are these people picky, picky, picky—or is there a sensory reason for their food fanaticism?

As a registered/certified occupational therapist, I've seen hundreds of children who had difficulty with eating and other related problems. Here are several examples that show why eating is an important foundational experience.

Five-year-old Darien would eat only spicy chicken wings. He liked both the intensity of taste and the bite-sized portion. For Darien, chicken wings were consistently dependable and offered some sensory satisfaction. All other food options were spit out—or thrown across the room!

Darien needed therapeutic intervention to be able to better define what was happening inside his mouth. Darien was using the sharp spice flavor to help him feel the boundaries on the inside of his mouth.

On the other hand, Julie was extremely sensitive to textures and flavors in foods. This four-year-old would eat only bland "real" mashed potatoes. She could tell the difference in potatoes that were not made "fresh," and she would hurl them across the room if what her mother put on her plate weren't freshly cooked and mashed!

Her parents were worried about nutrition. Her brothers and sisters weren't able to take an extended trip with Julie, because her parents weren't certain they could find potatoes to her liking in their constantly changing surroundings. Julie often stayed with an aunt while the rest of the family went on vacation, bonding and creating memories without her.

Unlike Darien, Julie's mouth was overly sensitive. She needed therapeutic intervention to make her mouth less sensitive so that she could tolerate foods with different temperatures and textures.

Six-year-old Candie would stuff her mouth with whatever food was placed in front of her. She didn't choke, but her parents and teachers were concerned that she might.

Like Darien, she could not locate the boundaries of her mouth, so she stuffed her mouth in an effort to find them. She used volume of food instead of spice to help her find those boundaries.

When I began to work with each of these children, I found the following regimen of *oral-motor desensitization/oral-motor facilitation* useful in helping them conquer their challenges. **Please note that oral-motor facilitation requires specialized training and is not recommended therapy to be attempted by a parent or teacher.**

With a gloved hand, I massage gums and cheeks and introduce cheek, lip, and tongue exercises. I exercise extreme caution—

being bitten is a real occupational hazard for the occupational therapist! Children who are sensitive are not always fond of manipulation in their mouths and facial area.

Each child is different, and it's impossible to tell ahead of time how much therapy will be needed. Some cases are solved with one or two therapeutic sessions; others take daily sessions over an extended period of time. Parent participation, a home program, and sometimes behavior modification are integral parts of the treatment plan.

What were the results with my three young students? Darien and Julie went on to eating and enjoying all types of foods. Eventually we became concerned about too much weight gain! In addition to an oral-motor program, Candie also needed a behavior-modification program to help her learn to deal appropriately with food offered to her. However, in time she too was able to eat in a safe and pleasurable fashion.

Five-year-old Hannah would chew on everything she could get her mouth on! Her sleeves and collars were developing holes where she gnawed on them. She'd put inedible objects—such as buttons and small rocks—in her mouth to explore their textures. After initially chewing gum, she'd soon swallow it.

Her parents realized that it was important to get this behavior under control as soon as possible, because once inappropriate chewing becomes a habit, it becomes more difficult to manage. I worked with her mother to analyze Hannah's problem. As part of the solution, her mother started serving foods that offered more texture. She made these substitutions to the family's diet:

- Raw or lightly blanched vegetables instead of canned

- Bagels and multi-grain breads (sometimes toasted) rather than soft white bread

- Al dente pasta (pasta boiled and taken out before it becomes too soft) in place of canned noodle dinners

- Firm fruit such as fresh apples, pears, and melon and chewy dried fruit such as raisins, cherries, and apricots rather than sauced fruit and fruit juices

- Crisp, crunchy finger foods, such as crackers, pretzels, bread sticks, and low-sugar cookies and cereals rather than soft cakes, pies, ice cream, and donuts

- Crunchy rather than creamy peanut butter

With limited therapeutic intervention and a consistent home program, Hannah's need to chew inappropriately decreased. By the time she was in first grade her collars and sleeves looked like those of her classmates—and she no longer felt the need to put buttons and pebbles into her mouth.

Many children munch their food (up and down movement of upper and lower teeth) and have very little rotary jaw movement and/or tongue action inside the mouth. Food has very little taste when it just sits in the mouth. Try putting a bite of gelatin on your tongue without moving it around. Not much happening, is there? Might even want to spit it out?

We use our mouth, lips, tongue, teeth, and the ability to chew and swallow to allow us the pleasure of tasting and enjoying our food. Many children do not have the ability to enjoy their food in these ways. As a result, they will choose to eat foods that go along with their method of compensating. When the *oral-motor area* (area inside and/or around the mouth) is either too sensitive or has no feeling, the child's food preferences reflect the method of compensating and managing the challenge.

The tongue, lips, and chewing pattern are usually underutilized in children with difficulty in the oral-motor area. Try making a variety of movements with your lips (the vowel sounds, a kiss, mama). Now try licking your lips and touching your tongue to each side of your mouth. Lick something outside your mouth, like a soft-serve cone. You'll probably see and feel use of these structures within normal limits, but many children with challenges in this area don't.

The tongue is especially important in managing and tasting foods. Once again, imagine eating gelatin without using your tongue to manipulate the bite of food, called a *bolus*. Now imagine trying to eat raisins with an up and down bite pattern (*munch*), rather than using rotary jaw movement with tongue action that flips the bite around in your mouth. We rarely think about these things, and they can have a huge impact on performance and enjoyment. No wonder food is not a high priority for children with oral-motor challenges!

Children with feeding concerns may also have difficulty with washing their faces and brushing their teeth. They're so sensitive that they won't allow the brush in their mouths, and there can be a gigantic power struggle to get this basic oral hygiene accomplished.

Every night Jill's mom and dad dreaded the fight that would ensue when it came time to brush her teeth. And she became extremely upset when the dentist needed to examine her mouth.

Andy's mom and dad weren't able to get anything that remotely resembled a toothbrush near him, much less in his mouth.

Babysitters knew not to attempt the project, lest the rest of the evening become a disaster.

The good news is that, in many cases, the toothbrushing challenge can be solved! I've found a therapeutic program implementing oral-motor desensitization very helpful with children such as Jill and Andy. Several techniques can help give the child a feeling of controlling the situation:

- Working with the child while standing behind him

- Using a small hand mirror to show the child the inside of her mouth

- Using rubber-tipped brushes to help massage the gums

- Allowing the child to hold the brush with the adult's hand on top to guide

- Using a variety of flavors and foods to enhance lip and tongue action

After several oral-motor desensitization sessions, little Lizzy would actually come to me and take my index finger to indicate that she was ready to brush her teeth and needed my assistance. That represented a major victory for her family, believe me!

Eating should be a joy the whole family shares together. If dinnertime is like a battle zone at your house, please take action to get professional help. I've seen real miracles happen in this area—sometimes in a very short time!

Chapter Ten

The Nose Knows
Smells Trigger Memories. . .Good and Bad

The sense of smell is immensely influential in our lives, and many times we don't even realize it! Many times odors can trigger memories faster than any other type of stimulus.

Dana and Chuck were in the market to buy a home. They were desperate for an appointment to see what they both agreed was a charming house, just what they were looking for. After considerable trouble, the real estate agent was finally able to coordinate schedules to get into the house. The key to the front door wasn't available, so the agent took them in the house through the back door, directly into the kitchen. Dana and Chuck hurried through the house, asking no questions, and then quickly said no to purchasing the home.

The agent couldn't understand their negative reaction, since they liked the outside of the home so much. No one could put a finger on what happened. Later, when Dana and Chuck sat down to talk about it, they realized that the smell of simmering cabbage permeated the house. This pungent odor—which conjured unpleasant memories for them both—was the first thing they noticed when they entered the kitchen. The sense of smell (*olfactory system*) triggered a "leave-now" response in them, and they lost all interest in that house.

On the other hand, fragrances sometimes assist in home sales—fresh flowers on the table, potpourri in the bathroom, and the scent of apple pie or cinnamon rolls wafting from the kitchen. (If your home is for sale, try it—you may be pleasantly surprised!)

The brain quickly interprets information about smell. This assessment often takes place below a level of conscious thinking (*subcortical*). Odors are categorized into three areas: as safe; to be avoided; or dangerous—prepare for immediate action!

Conjure up the first whiff of spring and the fresh-cut grass, a turkey roasting to a golden brown in the oven, ruby-red spaghetti sauce simmering on the stove (another clue that I am Italian and like to eat), or fluffy popcorn topped with golden butter available at the movies. Recently a woman cried when the theater concession ran out of fresh-popped popcorn. Who knows what the sensory implications were to raise that kind of reaction in her!

Consider the possibility of being overwhelmed by the scent of flowers at a funeral, sour milk on the carpet, a litter box that hasn't been cleaned in weeks, or neglected livestock stalls. Memories flood the system when the sense of smell "remembers" the significant details that are attached to those odors. The magnitude of the scents and their importance varies with the experiences to which they are attached for each individual person. For example, when our family visited the petting farm with our young children, my first aromatic impression was "Ugh!" and my husband's was "Ahhhh!"

Think about the scent of pine and how that brings up thoughts of the holidays. For some people that is good, but for others it may evoke sad or anxious feelings. Differing associations are made—based on experience—when people are faced with scents in their environment perceived as sensory input to be avoided. Hospitals and restaurants, for example, often request that their employees not wear fragrances for this very reason. Now think about how your body reacts to the odor of fire or hot electric wires and the smell of a gas leak. We have a survival orientation for detection of danger.

As one of our most primitive senses, the olfactory system helps us to seek pleasure, avoid pain, and sense danger. When five-year-old Lea was introduced to new situations, she'd sniff objects and people around her. Her parents tried to avoid new experiences because her unusual behavior made them uneasy. Lea was using her keen sense of smell to determine her level of safety and to help organize herself in new surroundings. She was using sensory systems in a way that was meaningful to her. Once she was involved in a professional program to mature sensory-motor processing, she stopped inappropriate sniffing.

Messages about the odors around you are making impressions of experiences, even when you don't realize it. When you're confused as to why you feel a certain way, take an in-depth look at what you're smelling and what might be happening to trigger memories that are anchored in the past.

We're beginning to explore the olfactory system and the power that drives it. At this point, we're probably seeing only the tip of the iceberg—undoubtedly there is much more beneath the surface. Today we're surrounded by an abundance of aromatherapy products, perfumed lotions and oils, and potpourri. Products such as these lend themselves to reaching us through both the senses of touch and smell. For many people these can enhance the quality of their lives.

A child who becomes extremely upset when faced with odors might be demonstrating sensory defensiveness in this area. Sensory defensiveness is an inclination to overreact to sensory input that would usually be considered unoffending. (See the chapter "Sensory Deficits.") In this therapist's opinion, professional treatment would begin with the Wilbarger Approach to Treating Sensory Defensiveness, which is explained in that chapter.

Don't assume that everybody will respond in the way you do to smells! Remember that the nose of another may know something you don't about the personal processing of sensory information.

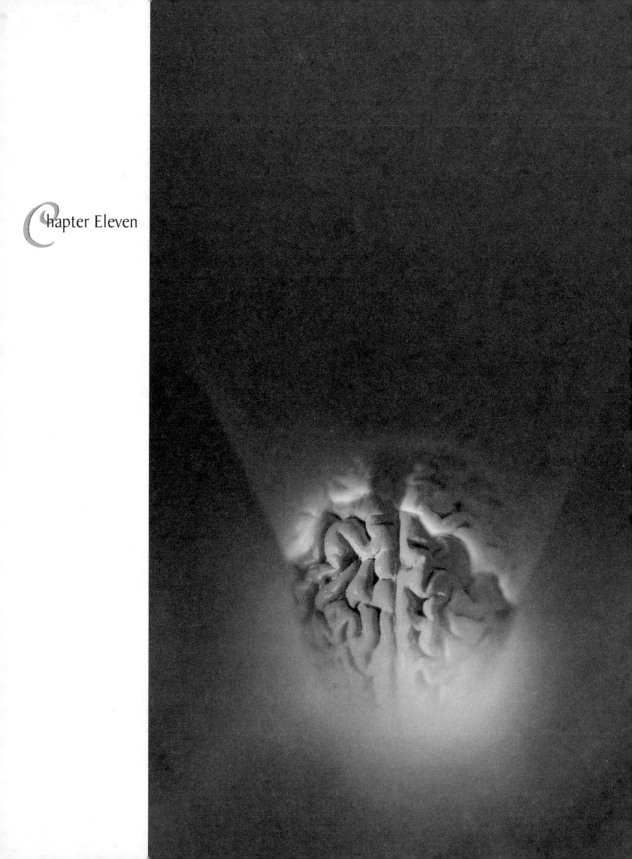

Chapter Eleven

Sensory Experiences & Academics
What's the Connection?

Parents and teachers frequently ask me how sensory-motor processing is related to academics, usually considered the basics of the school experience. Moving, touching, matching, sorting, classifying, playing, and socializing are considered appropriate programming in preschool and kindergarten. But they're often treated as enrichment exercises that aren't necessary once "real" school starts.

The activities that children engage in prepare them for life. In *Parenthood by Proxy: Don't Have Them If You Won't Raise Them*, Dr. Laura Schlessinger writes, "Children are most absorbed by situations in which they can express themselves and discover something about the world. That is why pots and pans and everyday things in drawers can engross a child for hours as they come up with new uses for mundane objects—the function of which they may not even know....The key to healthy development in children is providing opportunities for them to experience an expansive universe and affect it. Perpetual stimulation is dulling. Action is perpetually thrilling."[5]

Too many challenges in foundational skills—or not allowing children enough time to experience and internalize skills necessary to form a firm foundation—create situations which force children to use thinking skills when responses should be occurring automatically. Our bodies have a number of automatic functions—breathing, digesting food, eliminating toxins from our bodies, and so forth. A person can have problems in any of these areas. Likewise, sensory-motor-processing and sensory integration usually take place automatically. But a person can have problems in these areas, too. Parents and educators who pay attention to the development of strong foundational skills can help children with learning challenges more easily cross the bridge into academics.

In her book *Smart Moves: Why learning Is Not All in Your Head*, Carla Hannaford, Ph.D., neurophysiologist and educator writes, "Experiences and sensations *are* learning. Sensations form the base understanding from which concepts and thinking develop. Sensory enriched environments are imperative to learning...."[6]

Let me illustrate the link between foundational skills and more complex learning with examples of real children. When four-year-old Andrew manipulates sensory material, he is developing finger control, eye-hand coordination, and hand-to-hand coordination. As he completes a textured puzzle of a puppy, he's using vision that is immediately in front of him (*focal vision*) while strengthening his sense of discriminating awareness (*tactile system*).

Janice uses her hands and develops her sense of touch when she pours water and fills different-sized containers. But she's also using her brain to mentally manipulate objects in space (*space visualization*). These are prerequisites to abstract thought. As she matures, her ability to think about a math problem and to solve it in her head can be strengthened because of her playing with water and cups.

Social skills are developed as Jamie plays cooperatively with others, shares, and takes turns. This helps him to become less egocentric, more capable of abstract thought.

When Ryan and David play, they learn to use visual-perceptual skills, including recognizing similar versus different characteristics, improving visual memory, recognizing the important figure in a conglomerate, and determining the constancy of shape, size, and form of various objects.

Patti must understand the idea that something can represent a concept before she begins to read, since letters and words are a code that will eventually represent ideas. This concept is strengthened as she uses sensory material in dramatic play.

Scott develops problem-solving skills when utilizing a variety of materials for his own purposes. He learns by getting an idea, structuring that idea, and then following through with it.

Science concepts and the scientific process of inquiry are developed as Tony experiments with a variety of ideas and uses trial and error to discover firsthand the physical properties of the materials he's using.

Math skills are developed as Leslie pours and measures beans, rice, sand, dried peas, cereal, water, and juice into different-sized containers. She uses quantitative language to compare which holds more, less, or equal amounts, and compares weight and volume.

The children in these illustrations were all successful in learning. But what about a child who is challenged? Here's the story of one eight-year-old.

First thing every school morning Gerri would listen intently to the teacher, resolved to do better than she did yesterday. But soon she had trouble following the teacher's instructions. The teacher said to make four columns by folding a piece of paper into fourths. She then told the students to place all of the work written on the board in blue in the first column, pink in the second, yellow in the third, and green in the fourth.

Gerri completely missed the instructions about color and columns—she's still trying to fold the paper correctly! This child has to use a lot more energy than her peers to figure out how to fold the paper in the direction that the teacher had in mind, to be able to see the almost invisible lines that the folds made to create columns (*figure-ground-perception*), to match, sort, and classify the colors that the teacher had scattered all over the board. She also has a difficult time finding the dark green letters on the blackboard.

But Gerri has an additional sensory roadblock. Her desk is by the window, and when the 9 o'clock train rushes by (several blocks away), her sensory processing (*auditory figure ground*) does not allow two competitive sounds to make sense simultaneously. For Gerri, the train doesn't fade into the background—it drowns out what the teacher is saying. By now she's totally lost, and her teacher thinks she's not paying attention. No wonder Gerri has a hard time in class, and often goes home with a note from the teacher concerning her behavior.

After a consultation regarding sensory processing, the teacher began to understand what Gerri was up against. She did the following to help Gerri and other children having difficulty in her class:

- She used a visual demonstration of how she wanted a project done and placed it on a high easel for all to see.

- In addition to the oral directions, she also printed her directions with white chalk on the upper left side of the blackboard (creating greater contrast and consistency) for children who needed to refresh their memory, or for those who came in late.

- She used better voice projection and stopped talking when other interfering noises interrupted her instruction to students. When she began again, she quickly summarized and then went on with further instruction.

- She moved Gerri's desk to the other side of the room so that she was as far as possible from inside interference (heating/cooling system) and outside noise (playground, traffic, train). She made sure that the windows were closed during tests.

- She told Gerri that she could raise her hand for additional help anytime she felt overwhelmed. In addition the teacher assigned students as "peer pals" (who were able to raise their own self-esteem) to help Gerri. An added benefit was that Gerri, a shy child, was able to develop friendships outside of school.

When we examine foundational skills, we learn that the first level of maturation involves taking in and detecting information. If information doesn't make sense or is noxious to the system, it will either be avoided or ignored. Gerri's teacher used sensory techniques to help her struggling student. Soon Gerri was able to understand and follow instructions and concentrate on her schoolwork.

Even earlier intervention can be helpful for some children. Two-year-old Dwight would stand at the window—staring at nothing in particular—arms up, hands flapping back and forth at eye level. His mother was very concerned because he didn't make sounds and she couldn't engage him in purposeful activity or even get him to look at her. Dwight was stuck at the first level on the Foundational Skills Inventory and could not detect and process sensory information. He needed therapeutic intervention to "wake up" his system so he could begin to register information.

Children who don't participate in recess or who have difficulty with classes that are usually considered fun might be broadcasting signals for help. Watch and listen to the behavior that children engage in repeatedly. Attempt to understand what the child is trying to tell you, possibly in the only way she knows how. Remember, use behavior as a form of "secret" communication.

If you've noticed unusual behavior but can't identify exactly what is wrong, please get professional help. A sensory-motor history and evaluation may be the first step in changing a child's life—and ultimately benefiting family dynamics.

Contact the special education director in your home district or intermediate school district for help in finding a trained professional for evaluation or consultation. Many hospitals have outpatient therapy departments; some private clinics specialize in evaluation, consultation, home programs, and treatment. For additional information contact: American Occupational Therapy Association, Inc. (See "Additional Resources" at the end of this book for contact information.)

Chapter Twelve

Sensory Deficits
Finding out What's Wrong

At times, behaviors that are based on sensory deficits or sensory needs might look like intentionally negative behaviors. Children who demonstrate difficulty with sensory motor processing have an impaired ability to make use of sensory input that would enable them to generate automatic responses. It is becoming more of a common problem, and is often missed.

This type of disorder can have profound influence on development because it interferes with learning, using social skills, and communicating with others. It can be difficult to test children with severe sensory-processing challenges because it is often hard for them to tolerate the test situation or understand what is expected of them to answer and/or perform correctly.

Difficulty with sensory motor processing and sensory integration has little to do with intelligence, although underlying abilities can be hidden by the inability to organize and process information. Parents and teachers may have a sense that something isn't right, but usually aren't able to pinpoint what it is. The child's actions can appear to indicate a behavior problem, and are often treated with Applied Behavior Analysis (ABA). (Note: A person can be deficient in several of these areas but may have learned to compensate for his deficiencies. In such cases, intervention might not be necessary, but making good choices is enhanced with understanding.)

Children may have a cluster of indicators pointing to a challenge. Some of these behaviors might include:

- Difficulty paying attention—doing the same thing over and over (*distractible/perseverating*)

- Fixating—focusing on one thing for an extended period

- Activity level inappropriately too high or too low

- Avoiding movement or touch

- Difficulty maintaining alertness—frequent need to rest on arms, put head on desk, etc.

- Unpredictable (*labile*) emotions (outbursts for no apparent reason)

- Difficulty interacting successfully or appropriately with other people

- Difficulty adjusting to change in routine

- Difficulty organizing self/environment and using self-control

- Difficulty concentrating and using reasoning skills

- Poor self-confidence

- Diminished capacity for abstract thought

Sensory defensiveness is an inclination to overreact to sensory input that would usually be considered acceptable. It can occur in a variety of areas—including avoidance of touch, avoidance of certain foods, irrational fear in change of position (fear of being upside down, putting head backwards, leaving the ground, etc.), and fear of certain noises. It becomes a major concern when it directs behavior. Many times sensory defensive behavior can control the household and everyone in it.

This type of sensory deficit requires therapeutic intervention consisting of a sensory history, evaluation, treatment, and a program overseen by a professional trained in this area. I have used the Wilbarger Approach to Treating Sensory Defensiveness with great success. This is an intensive technique accomplished with a deep pressure device (a special clear plastic therapy device). This program requires participation and dedication for all concerned. With this approach, the defensiveness can be reduced or eliminated. In many cases, the results are nothing short of a miracle!

Getting ready for school was a difficult time for five-year-old Deanna and her entire family. Screaming sessions were the norm before dressing. She would wear only one outfit to school and would wear only her boots, without socks. (At other times outfits that she might tolerate would have to be extra large on her.) Her older brother was always late to school because they had to walk together.

After a few weeks of intensive occupational therapy using the Wilbarger Approach to Treating Sensory Defensiveness, screaming sessions were history and Deanna became fond of skipping to school—early! Two weeks later she was in a fashion show, trying on all kinds of outfits and modeling them with pride! Within a month Deanna's entire life changed. Four years later, she proudly displayed an outfit of turtleneck and jeans to the occupational thera-pist who treated her. What a thrill for everyone!

Most people have some degree of control over themselves and can learn to pay attention. *Self-regulation* is the ability to recognize arousal states as they relate to paying attention, learning, and behavior. Mary Sue Williams and Sherry Shellenberger, occupational therapists, have written about how we (usually automatically) regulate the state of alertness for activity. "Self-Regulation is the ability to attain, maintain, and change arousal appropriately for a task or situation....When we think of all the things we hope for our children...we assume that they will be able to listen to us, to attend for a period of time, and to be calm enough or awake enough to participate in learning experiences....The Alert Program [for self-regulation]…encourages the use of sensorimotor strategies to manage our levels of alertness."[7]

Many people automatically do something that helps them to regulate their level of alertness in order to focus. Some of these strategies include: chewing gum, sucking on candy, crunching on a snack, biting fingernails, whistling, drinking caffeinated beverages, eating sour or spicy foods, biting lips, twisting a lock of hair, drumming fingers, watching a fire in a fireplace or fish in an aquarium, doing exercise, and dancing.

If you think that your child may have a problem with sensory integration, you may want to consider looking into an occupational therapy evaluation based on a sensory history and sensory motor processing/sensory integration. (Dr. Lucy Miller's research and websites are extremely valuable—see Additional Resources page 143.) This information could make all the difference in the world in your child's ability to function and enjoy life!

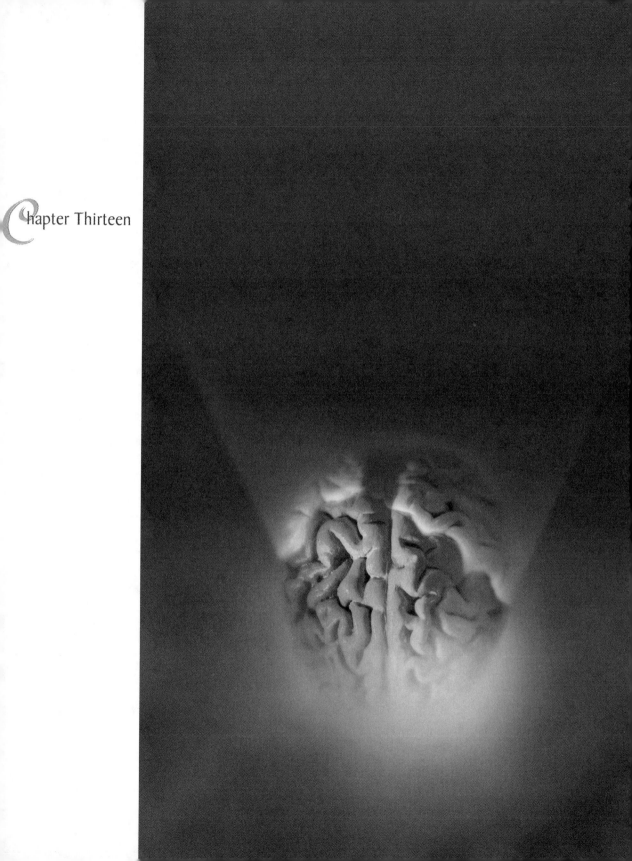

Chapter Thirteen

Creating a Sound Sensory Diet
It's as Important as Good Nutrition!

Parents and teachers are eager to enhance the lives of children, but sometimes they need hands-on information to help them get started with improving a sensory diet. Here are some ideas, most of which are easy to implement. Pick and choose the ones that will fit into your family's (or classroom's) program.

Note: Children with physical or other health impairments and/or seizure disorder must be involved with a qualified therapist in creating an appropriate sensory diet.

Many children at play will move toward creating their own sensory diets, involving a variety of exploring and moving. They unconsciously include muscle action and tactile experiences. Although they don't understand what they're doing, they'll often come up with quite a good mix on their own.

When the parent or teacher understands the importance of the foundational skills and the child exhibits minimal immaturity, things to remember include introducing new activities, and allowing ample time for children to explore, organize, and integrate their experiences. In a word, make sure that the child has time to **play**.

A therapist trained in sensory motor processing should be consulted if the child is having considerable difficulty in any of these areas:

- Over-sensitivity to sensory stimulation

- Under-sensitivity to sensory stimulation

- Inability to process information (looks like avoidance)

- Inability to organize (looks like disorganization, lack of self-control, activity level too high/too low, poor capacity for abstract thought)

- Avoiding sensory information

- Physical impairment with or without a seizure disorder

In some cases, a home and school program specifically designed to meet the needs of the child's nervous system with a selected sensory diet will suffice; in other cases, therapy is indicated. If you're concerned with a child's ability to make sense of the world around him, I urge you to seek out an occupational therapy consultation with a registered/certified professional.

The next pages provide examples of activities that can help to provide a sensory diet for most non-handicapped children. **Remember to supervise activity and make sure that it's safe and appropriate for the age level and physical ability of the child.** Be sure to include a variety in each day's activities! These suggestions will get you started. Play with the children; you might enjoy it more than you think!

Activities Involving Movement and Joint Action

- Exercising to music—include walking, running, galloping, skipping, jumping, and hopping

- Engaging in household activities that involve pushing, pulling, squeezing, lifting, carrying, twisting, and lugging. Include in the child's sensory diet chores such as vacuuming, climbing the stairs to find and empty the wastebaskets upstairs, making the bed, carrying groceries, helping to move light furniture, helping to set the table, raking leaves, watering flowers, digging in the garden, and carrying the laundry basket, folding, and putting away clothes

- Jumping activities, including traditional jump rope, jumping over a rope placed on the floor, walking between rungs of a "ladder" created by using colored tape on the floor, hopscotch, jumping over lines on the sidewalk, and using a trampoline (in safe situations)

- Playing games in a gym class, including soccer, basketball, volleyball, tennis, tag, tug-of-war, playing catch with a variety of objects (Frisbee, bean bags, balls of various sizes, weights, and textures)

- Sledding, roller or ice skating, gymnastics, tap dancing, and ballet

- Using playground equipment involving swinging, rocking, climbing, hanging safely from bars, teeter-totter, merry-go-round

- Riding tricycles, bicycles or scooters

- Walking on a balance beam, the lines on the sidewalk, on sand dunes and the beach

- Dancing with a variety of moves, including twirling, wiggling, and shaking the body.

Activities Involving Touch and Joint Interaction

Introduce children to a variety of textures whenever possible during the course of daily living experiences. Here are some ideas:

- While on an outing, feel the dirt, hug a tree, pick a blade of grass, play on the beach, make sand castles.

- Let your child help with safe cooking tasks, such as preparing vegetables, squeezing and shaping dough, taking seeds out of a pumpkin.

- Rub lotion on the hands and body.

- Play in the snow (dressed in appropriate clothing).

- Splash in a swimming pool (under supervision).

- Play musical instruments such as bongo drums, rhythm sticks, tambourine, piano, sand blocks, bells, and cymbals.

- Play with objects and toys such as squishy squeeze

balls, laser-spinning tops, finger puppets, kneadable erasers, foam blocks, Legos, and magnet toys.

- Play with clay, beads, beans, shells, feathers, rubber bands, craft supplies, finger paints, bubbles, and squirt toys.

- Use hand and finger punches; pick up small objects with tweezers.

- Care for family pets—bathing, brushing, feeding, exercising and cleaning a cage or pen.

- Sleep under flannel sheets, snuggle under blankets, make a bed tent, use an oversized sheet to tuck under the mattress to create a tight-fitting cocoon.

- Observe and discuss temperature variables such as the difference between cool and cold, lukewarm and warmer. Show variations in touch. Demonstrate pressure, such as light touch (pat on the back) and deep touch (hug).

- Become aware of clothing preferences, such as a dislike of headbands and hats; desire to wear heavy materials such as denim or spandex; or wanting to wear light-weight down jackets and sleeveless tops. Discuss whether the child prefers to go barefooted or keep her shoes on.

- Identify items without using vision. For example, have the child place his hands behind his back and place an object on his upturned palm. Set a time limit to increase the fun. This is increasing *stereognostic* abilities.

- Play games where letters and numbers are "drawn" with finger on another's back. This increases *graphesthesia* abilities.

Using Mouth and Nose

(Always Remember: Safety is our main concern.)

- Introduce foods that have a variety of textures, flavors, consistencies, and spiciness. (Consult a professional if child resists or if there is danger of choking)

- Include in your family's diet foods that require sucking, licking, chewing over a longer period, biting, and crunching. Encourage discussion about which kinds of food each member of the family prefers.

- Teach your children to sing, hum, whistle, and play with blow toys (such as a harmonica).

- Make the child more aware of scents by talking about taking deep breaths and encouraging her to discover and talk about the similarities and differences of scents. The kitchen is a good place to discuss favorite smells.

Using Ears

- Use music as a background to another activity. Vary the tempo to conform to the mood that is desired (e.g. quiet, relaxing music shortly before bedtime or a quick-paced tempo to generate enthusiasm for picking up toys scattered around the playroom).

- Become aware of background noise and its effect on performance. Notice how the unexpected sound of an airplane, train, thunderstorm, barking dog, screech on blackboard, rhythmic sound of the heating or cooling system, phone ringing, dishwasher humming, or washing machine vibrating affect the concentration of your child. Notice what is comforting to his system and what is irritating.

- Notice how voice tone affects the child. Become aware of differences in quality of whispers and listen to variations in volume and intensity (e.g. squealing for joy on the playground compared to screaming in fright).

Using Eyes

- Observe the child's ability to follow a moving object without moving his head (*tracking*).

- Develop awareness of the quality of light on productivity, such as fluorescent light, dim and bright light, sunlight, shadow.

- Watch the effects of color—the color of the room where working, intensity of color in objects around the child, choice of color for her clothing. What increases work output—lots of bright primary color or a plain, neutral background?

- Become aware of the amount of simplicity or clutter that is in the child's surroundings and how visual performance changes when a messy room is cleaned up—or a Spartan area is decorated with eye-catching objects.

- Play with a flashlight in a darkened room; create designs with lighted peg toys; push a sparkle wheel using finger strength to create sparks.

- Make shapes, numbers, letters, and pictures with a variety of materials; create a collage of different materials; put together jigsaw puzzles.

- Discuss same and different aspects of objects. Play a game to find a designated shape, such as a circle. Your child may see a clock, the bottom of a vase, a jar lid, and a round table. This simple activity challenges him to see a form and to find it even when the form is smaller, larger, rotated, reversed, or hidden in objects in the room. You can even play this game on a long car or plane trip.

- Draw, follow dot-to-dot pictures, and complete mazes.

- Do all kinds of crafts with a variety of textured materials—cut, paste, string beads, and make bows. Create designs on pegboards and duplicate them on another board.

- Match, sort, and classify objects and play games that involve doing so.

- Play card games.

- Encourage everyday activities that involve mentally manipulating objects in space, such as figuring out (in your head) which would be the proper size container for the leftover mashed potatoes. Have the child put away the food and see how he did. Pretend to rearrange the furniture in your child's room or redecorate the family room. Will all the furniture fit in the suggested arrangement?

- Find hidden objects in pictures. This develops the ability to perceive a form visually, and to find that form hidden in a conglomerated ground of matter.

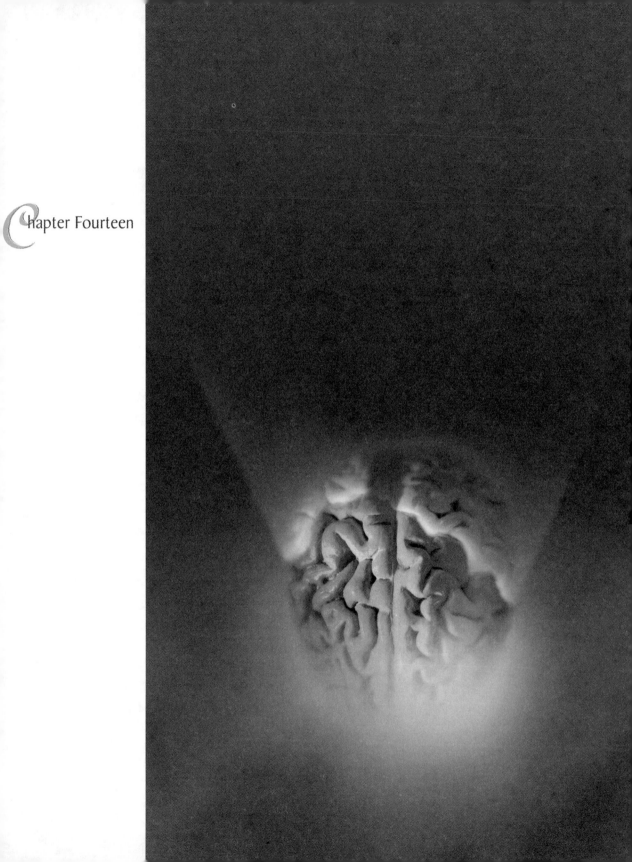

Chapter Fourteen

Foundational Skills Inventory
Putting This Tool to Work for You

Pay attention to your children. Take yourself out of the middle of a situation and observe!

Behavior is an important form of communication. In many cases, actions do indeed speak louder than words. Become aware of actions—and the cause and effect of the exhibited behaviors—from an objective point of view.

As you begin to observe more objectively, you may want to ask yourself the following questions:

- Does your child have lots of opportunity to move around?

- Do you use touch to comfort by giving appropriate hugs, lotion rubs, and massage?

- Are beanbags or pillows available for use on your floor?

- Does your child love to push a filled child's cart at the grocery store?

- Does she play in the mud and get covered with sand at the beach?

- Do you let him turn your garden hose on full-force and play in the water?

- Does your child experience different textures by playing with pebbles, rice, beans, and dry noodles? (**Note: Do not use small objects with young children or developmentally delayed children who might choke on them.**)

- Does your child crave activities that require exertion, such as pushing, pulling, lugging, carrying, and lifting?

Your child might be "asking" for more opportunities to feel and to move. Children progress toward what they need to make their bodies function optimally. But if they do the same thing over and over with little satisfaction—or when they have little opportunity to move, touch, and safely explore their world—challenges might be around the corner.

I've created some tools that can help parents and teachers find out more about a child's foundational skills. First, become acquainted with the page entitled Foundational Skills in a Nutshell (page 35). This sheet can give you an idea of what the progressive levels of skills look like, without the detail. It is a general chart to familiarize you with the concept.

As parents and educators, understanding the neurological need for movement, joint interaction, and touch is critical. The Foundational Skills Inventory (found on the inside back cover) helps to detail—quickly and efficiently—the specific areas of need. The Inventory has been devised as an all-inclusive tool that can be completed with what you already know about the child. Another way to use it is to observe and record information over a period of time.

Children must detect and take in information before they can learn. The foundational skills build upon each other and optimize learning opportunities. When there are too many holes in the foundation, forcing a child to learn can be a traumatic experience.

Earlier in this book you met Dwight, who would stand by the window staring out into space, flapping his hands. He was in an "avoidance" mode of learning—he didn't have the ability to take in and use information. Therefore he couldn't organize information or be involved with skills needed for higher learning—skills such as matching, sorting, classifying, and realizing the same and different aspects of objects. All these skills lead up to differentiating letters prior to reading.

Dwight wasn't able to pay attention to learn specific skills for tasks like feeding or dressing himself, developing social skills, or interacting with people while accomplishing a complex task. The Inventory could help Dwight's mother identify her son's problem areas. When she looked at the levels on the Foundational Skills Inventory, she could find clues about where to start working with Dwight before she obtained help from a registered occupational or licensed physical therapist trained in sensory motor processing/sensory integration. (Fortunately, Dwight did get the professional help he needed.)

The Foundational Skills Inventory can be used in a variety of ways:

- It can be used as a reference to realize the multitude of skills necessary to create a firm foundation for learning and to understand why some children behave the way that they do.

- A consulting or collaborating therapist can give parents and educators the Inventory to complete. This allows the therapist to begin the process of helping a child as soon as possible.

- Social workers, psychologists, educators, and therapists can use it to help document an alternative motivation for behaviors that—on the surface—appear to be noncompliant.

Initially the Inventory may look somewhat confusing. That's okay. It's good to have a feel for the quantity of information that we've been taking for granted. Once you take a good look at this chart and get used to the wealth of information presented, you'll be amazed at how it can help you. When you look at a completed Inventory for a child who has many challenges, you can actually see why her system is having a hard time coping with academics.

Are you ready to try using this tool yourself? Turn to the Foundational Skills Inventory (on the inside back cover of this book).

- Fill in today's date, and the name and birthdate of the person that you wish to inventory.

- Go to the bottom of the page. **Work each level from left to right, circling any statements that are true. Use a black felt-tip marker to darken any statement that is false.** Some of the sections are more technical and may be unfamiliar. If you feel unable to complete a section, you may choose to refer to the bibliography and read additional material or consult a professional for help. If all else fails, leave the areas blank. **Note: Remember that the Foundational Skills**

Inventory is based on developmental sequence and that young children will not go beyond the first levels.

When you've completed the exercise, you'll have a picture of one person's foundation for learning. Ideally, you'll have a sheet of paper with many thick black lines that represent steps to the top, where "academics" start. The circles represent "holes." When there are too many "holes" and not enough "steps" to get to the top, learning can be difficult.

Let me emphasize again that everyone has scattered "holes" in his foundational skills; that is to be expected. As adults, we compensate by avoiding these areas.

People who have serious foundational needs may respond in a variety of ways. Some common behaviors I've observed in the children I've worked with include:

- Some withdraw or appear depressed, avoiding that which is difficult.

- Some act out and are highly emotional.

- Others decide to become powerful in an area of strength and avoid that which is difficult.

I hope this tool is useful to you. The Foundational Skills Inventory is also available in multiple-sheet tablet form for those who wish to evaluate groups of children and/or retain evaluation records as part of permanent files. For many parents and professionals, it's a real eye-opener. If it's helpful to you, please contact me, I would like to hear of your success! (see Additional Resources, page 141).

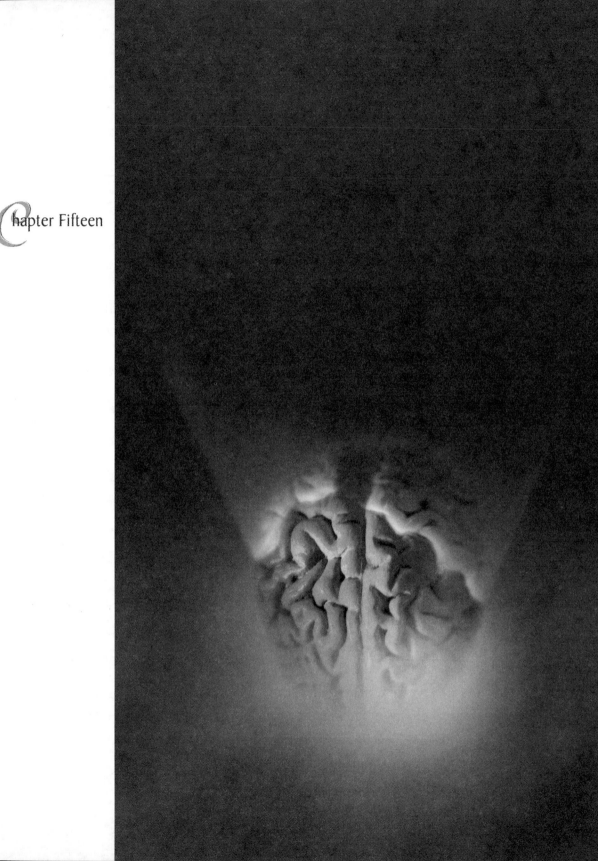

Chapter Fifteen

Here's Your Homework!
Preliminary Activities Can Jump-start Your Child's Academic Program

Parents and teachers often ask what they can do at home Notes while they're waiting for specific ideas following an occupational therapy evaluation. This chapter was written to meet that need. Most of these ideas aren't startling or new, and you may already know about them. These bulleted lists can provide quick reference and help you remember what you've already learned.

Important: If your child has a physical, mental, or seizure disorder, please check with your doctor before attempting these activities. My motto is, "If in doubt...don't." Remember that all activities for young children should be supervised for safety. Don't use small objects with young or developmentally delayed children who might choke on them. Become aware of the possibility of allergic reactions when using new materials with children.

Parents are the primary educators of their children. Building a strong foundation for learning begins at home. Sensory input from the skin and joints helps to develop body awareness.

Provide stimulation throughout the day by appropriate touching, hugging, rubbing, scratching, and kissing. Mention and play games that involve learning where body parts are located (*body concept*) and where body parts are in relation to position in space (*body schema*). Make bath time fun by using a variety of textured toys. Use towels that have different textures and are different colors. Ask which ones your child prefers. Remember that bubbles in the bath provide "light touch" and may not be welcomed by all children.

Remember this sensory secret: whenever possible, incorporate two or more senses into one activity. For example, to expand what your children are learning as you work with them, use mirrors to enhance the sense of sight. Allow them to handle safe items under discussion. Use music without words as a background, and adjust the tempo to the activity.

The next few pages categorize activities that can help your child improve in important areas. Select ideas that are appropriate for your family, and over a period of time try some from each category.

Supervised, safe, strenuous play increases body awareness, improves balance, increases awareness of position in space, and strengthens muscles:

- Creeping/crawling on a variety of surfaces (e.g. carpet, grass, soft tile, sand)

- Practicing a variety of "walks," (e.g. duck walk, elephant walk)

- Riding a pony or a rocking horse

- Throwing to a target (e.g. ring toss, beanbag throw)

Muscle-strengthening activities involve pushing, pulling, twisting, lifting, and carrying:

- Playing supervised tug-of-war

- Using shovels and other digging tools

- Using a kid's "construction kit" with large nuts and bolts

- Playing with water and using small buckets, sponges, and dishcloths

- Providing paper to rip, crumple, and pick up with salad tongs

- Playing with clay, dough, putty (For great ideas refer to the art section of *Electric Bread*, cited in bibliography.)

- Playing with squeeze toys, such as frog that hops when a connected bulb is squeezed

Vigorous play involves the whole body:

- Swinging, climbing, tumbling, jumping

- Water play

- Climbing stairs or hiking on a well-marked trail

- Riding wheeled vehicles

- Ball games of all types

Obstacle courses develop motor planning, coordination, and strength:

- Climbing in and out of boxes

- Crawling under a table or around furniture

- Walking on a rope placed in a variety of positions

Teach the prepositional space concepts:

- Help your child to understands these words: over, under, up, down, near, on, across, off, over, through, above, against, and past.

- Invent games that involve following instructions and that incorporate a variety of concepts. Try saying, "**Walk past** the sandbox. **Jump over** the hose. Then **crawl under** the monkey bars."

Encourage large, free-flowing movement that involves the shoulders and elbows:

- Scribbling on large paper or newsprint

- Painting murals on shelf paper (on the floor or taped to a wall)

- Finger painting

- "Painting" the sidewalk with a bucket of plain water and brush or a paint roller

- Drawing large circles on the chalkboard

- Catching and throwing large balls

- Dancing while holding onto a crepe paper "ribbon"

- Twirling a jump rope

- Riding a scooter board on stomach and using arms to propel

Develop finger manipulation skills by promoting finger awareness and isolation of finger movement:

- Apply hand lotion to individual fingers.

- Play finger games or use finger puppets.

- Poke or push individual fingers into dough, putty, clay, and other resistive materials.

- Push button toys and doorbells.

- Open boxes.

- Build with blocks.

- Work puzzles.

- Wind an old-fashioned clock or windup toys.

- Choose clothing that buttons and shoes that need to be tied—and let the child dress himself.

- Fold paper and make paper projects.

- Let the child turn the pages of a book as you read aloud.

Teach precision handling:

- Pull off small pieces of dough, clay, putty and roll them into little balls.

- Turn knobs.

- Squirt water toys at a target.

- Mist plants with a spray bottle.

- String beads.

- Use a peg board.

- Remove small objects from a larger container using a pinch-type tool such as salad tongs.

- Snap fingers.

- Unwrap a piece of candy.

- Shuffle and fan playing cards.

- Remove coins from a purse.

- Spin tops.

- Twist pipe cleaners to create various shapes.

- Pick up raisins—one at a time—with the first three fingers, and then hold them with the last two fingers against the palm, while picking up more.

Practice improving joint stability within the hand:

- Hold plastic tableware while drying it with a dish towel.

- Support a cafeteria tray.

- Wring out wet cloths and sponges.

Teach safe use of scissors:

- Practice with tweezers as a preliminary tool for learning how to open and close blades.

- Use blunt-nosed scissors to snip straws, old playing cards, and the advertising insert cards from magazines.

- Practice snipping with scissors while touching the pads of the last two fingers to palm.

- Snip off corners following heavy lines you've drawn. As the child improves, make the lines lighter, curved, or closer to the middle of the paper.

As you begin to enjoy these activities with your children, you'll probably come up with dozens of other ideas. Most imporantly, have fun practicing the preliminary skills for academics with your children!

Always remember—time taken for our children is a very wise investment in our future! I challenge you to make a difference in the lives of our children—one child at a time!

Additional Resources

Abilitations
Early Intervention—Pediatric Equipment—Toys
www.abilitations.com

Abilities Center
Resource for Therapy, Workshops, Consultation
www.abilitiescenter.com

Achievement Products for Children
Specialty Products—Books
www.specialkidszone.com

ActiveForever, Inc.
Assistive Technology
www.ActiveForever.com

Alliance for Childhood
www.allianceforchildhood.net

American Occupational Therapy Association
www.aota.org (click on books and products)

Amazon
Books—Online Items
www.amazon.com

Avanti Educational Programs, Inc.
14547 Titus St., Suite 109, Van Nuys, CA 91402
(818) 782-7366 Fax: (818) 989-7826. (Information on Sensory
Defensiveness/Wilbarger.) Porsche Wilson, seminar coordinator:
Porsche@childdevmedia.com

Bal-A-Vis-X
Bill Hubert—Balance—Auditory—Visual—Exercises
www.bal-a-vis-x.com

Brain Highways
Research
www.brainhighways.com

Bright Tots
Educational Toys
www.brighttots.com

Brule
Native American Music
www.soundofamerica.com

Callirobics
Handwriting Exercises with Music
www.callirobics.com

Creative Therapy
Therapeutic Toys—Books—Games—Activities
www.creativetherapystore.com

Creative Teaching Tools
www.reallygoodstuff.com

Chudler, Dr. Eric
Neuroscience for Kids
http://faculty.washington.edu/chudler/tenper.html

Cross Country Education
Seminars—Workshops across the US
www.crosscountryeducation.com

Davies, Dr. Patti
Research—Brainwaves for Science
http://brainwaves.colostate.edu

Dining with Dignity
Elegant Flatware
www.diningwithdignity.com

Dore Center
Resources
www.dorecenter.com

Enabling Devices
Learning Devices
www.enablingdevices.com

Funtastic Learning
Educational Toys
www.funtasticlearning.com

Great Ideas
Personal Hygiene Assistive Products
www.solutioncomfortseat.com

Great Talking Box Company
Communication Aids
www.greattalkingbox.com

Harcourt Assessment, Inc.
Evaluation Tools
www.PsychCorp.com

Henry OT Services, Inc.
Sensory Integration—Sensory Processing
www.ateachabout.com

Independent Living Aids, Inc.
www.independentliving.com

Jump-In
Sensory Processing Products
www.jump-in-products.com

Kaye Products Inc.
Unique Therapy Products
www.kayeproducts.com

Miller, Dr. Lucy
Research—Kid Foundation
www.KIDFoundation.org
www.SPDnetwork.org

SPD Parent Connections
www.SPDnetwork.org/directory

Morris & Klein
Pre-Feeding Skills, 2nd Edition & Many Eating References
www.mealtimenotions.com

Pocket Full of Therapy
Unique Toys and Materials
www.pfot.com

Puppets 4U
www.puppets4U.com

Rescuing Recess
www.rescuingrecess.com

Sensory Integration Education & Research Foundation (SIERF)
www.sierf.org

Sensory Integration Focus Magazine
www.sifocus.com

Sensory Integration International
www.sensoryint.com

Sensory Secrets: How to Jump-Start Learning for Children
www.sensorysecrets.com

Special Populations
www.specialpopulations.com

Southpaw Enterprises, Inc.
www.southpawenterprises.com

The Concerned Group, Inc
Order Sensory Secrets
www.theconcernedgroup.com/sensorysecrets
(800) 447-4332

The Positive Difference, LLC
Dedicated to Excellence—Consultation/Presentations
Your Sensational Brain—Schneider & Poltorak
PosDiff@aol.com
www.sensorysecrets.com

The Speech Bin
www.speechbin.com

Therapy Shoppe
Hard-to-find items
www.TherapyShoppe.com

Therapy Skill Builders
Outstanding Gateway to Resources on the web
www.therapyskillbuilders.com

Therapy Works, Inc
Additional Excellent Gateway to Resources on the web
www.therapyworks.com

Wikki Stix Co.
Fine Motor Dexterity Material
www.wikkistix.com

Winning Topics Entertainment
Motivational Audio Materials
www.topics-ent.com
www.Fettke.com

Glossary

In an effort to make technical terms understandable to laypersons, I've taken the liberty of paraphrasing from resources common to occupational therapists. *Webster's Encyclopedic Unabridged Dictionary, Dorland's Illustrated Medical Dictionary, Sensory Integration: Theory and Practice* and *Advocate Newsletter—Autism Society of America* were used as references.

arousal: level of alertness appropriate to a situation and/or a task

auditory: referring to the act of hearing

auditory language processing: ability to understand spoken words

auditory discrimination: ability to recognize small changes in sounds; such as *b*a and *p*a

auditory-figure-ground discrimination: the ability to tune in to one source of sound, such as to listen to only one person talking in a noisy room

auditory memory: ability to remember what was heard

auditory perception: the process of hearing and understanding what was heard

auditory sequencing: the ability to remember, in order, a list of things heard

autism: a complex developmental disability that typically appears during the first three years of life. Autism is the result of a neurological disorder that affects the functioning of the brain and interferes with the normal development of social interaction and communication skills. A person with autism often exhibits difficulty in verbal, non-verbal communication, social interactions, and leisure or play activities.

Ayres, A. Jean, Ph.D., OTR, FAOTA: a brilliant woman who brought together her knowledge of neuroscience and occupational therapy to pioneer and create the theory, assessments, and treatment principles of sensory integration

bilateral: referring to both sides of the body

bilateral integration: coordination of the two sides of the body

brain stem: part of the brain that lies between the spinal cord and higher centers of the brain. Contains filtering system, which prioritizes incoming information to determine if it should be noticed or ignored.

central nervous system (CNS): the brain and network of nerves within the spinal cord which controls life functions, including movement and sensation

cerebellum: a portion of the brain serving to coordinate voluntary movements, posture, and balance; in back of and below the cerebrum

cerebrum: the large, outer part of the brain, consisting of two halves and serving to control voluntary movements and coordinate mental actions

closure: ability to recognize a whole, although one or more parts are missing

constancy: the quality of being unchanging; referring to form, shape, and/or size constancy

coordination: the ability to use muscles together in order to perform purposeful well-controlled movements

cortex: the outer layer of the brain; the convoluted layer of gray substance that covers each cerebral hemisphere

crossing the midline (CML): the ability to cross over the middle of the body easily, smoothly and automatically, usually with the arms and eyes

development: continual growth of the body and brain, physically, intellectually, socially, and emotionally

developmental delay: a term used to describe a child who is not able to do activities expected for his age in any particular area of development—physical, mental, social, emotional

developmental sequence: the order in which steps of development occur. The order of steps is fixed but can occur at different ages for different children. Average ages are often used as a guide to developmental age.

developmental therapy: a way of thinking about therapy which tries to take the child through the typical sequence of development

directionality: ability to relate the environment to oneself in terms of directions, such as, turn to the right, go under, get in front of

distal: refers to areas on the arms and legs which are farthest from the trunk (hands, fingers, feet)

dominance: ability to naturally perform better with one side of the body

epilepsy: a neurological disorder in which there are repeated instances of seizures; can often be controlled by medication

equilibrium reactions: automatic movements which give a person balance

eye-hand coordination: ability to coordinate vision with movement in general

facilitation: a kind of therapy technique used to make something possible or easier

figure-ground perception: ability to focus in on one thing without being distracted

fine motor: refers to activities that require coordination of small muscle movements, such as those in the hands and eyes

gait: the way in which someone walks, e.g. on her toes, pigeon-toed

gross motor: refers to activities which require coordination of large muscle movements, such as in walking, running, hopping, climbing

graphesthesia: the sense by which figures and or numbers are recognized when "written" on the skin

heavy touch: a term that occupational therapists use to indicate pressured touch that provides a localized, precise sensation that enables the person being touched to discriminate tactile awareness, e.g. determine shape, size, texture, etc.

heavy-work patterns: activity that helps to perceive joint and body movement as well as position of the body, or body segments, in space

hyperactive, hyperactivity: general terms that refer to a child who is excessively active and is unable to control it

hypertonic: referring to increased muscle tone (stiffness) which can limit both the variety and speed of movement; can lead to joint contractures

hypotonic: referring to decreased muscle tone which limits the ability to be stable and to hold positions for any length of time; can interfere with hand function because of poor shoulder control

kinesthetic: referring to sensation which provides information of muscle movement

labile: referring to rapid changes of moods, emotions, such as sudden, unexplained crying or laughing

language, expressive: ability to communicate an idea through speaking or writing

language, receptive: ability to understand an idea by listening or reading

laterality: ability to know the difference between right and left within the body

light touch: rapid, diffuse touch that has a spreading effect and alerts the nervous system to be aware of possible danger

motor planning: ability to sequence the movements required to do a specific, skilled activity

muscle tone: the amount of tension present in muscles; allows humans to remain upright against gravity

neurochemicals: chemicals called neurotrophins that act like fertilizer, nurturing the survival, development, and repair of neurons after they have been damaged. Scientists are finding that physical exercise creates these chemicals.

neurologist: a specialist in the diagnosis and treatment of disorders of the neuro-muscular system

neutral warmth: use of own body heat to bring about relaxation

neurology: the study of the network of the nerves and the brain

neuroscientists: researchers who are providing us with information regarding how basic, neural mechanisms of the central nervous system influence behavior and learning

occupational therapy: the therapeutic use of self-care, work, and play activities to increase independent function, enhance development, and prevent disabilities; may include adaptation of task or environment to achieve maximum independence and to enhance quality of life

ocular tracking: ability to follow a moving object with the eyes without moving the head

oculomotor: refers to movement and muscle control of the eyes

oral motor: refers to movement and muscle control of the mouth (lips, checks, tongue)

perception: process of organizing and interpreting sensory information, both from the environment and the body

perceptual motor: coordination of the perceptual experience and movement

perseveration: inappropriate repetition of an activity; e.g. in speech, scribbling, rocking, etc.

phonation: ability to make sounds

physical therapy: therapy that helps the child learn to move and develop gross motor skills; may provide consultation for positioning; can also work to help prevent deformities

physiology: science dealing with living organisms or their parts

position in space: ability to recognize and relate objects in the environment and self to environment in terms of orientation and organization; e.g. in front, behind, backwards

postural reactions: automatic muscle adjustments made to maintain a position

prone: lying on stomach

proprioception: perception of joint and body movement as well as position of the body in space

reflexes: automatic, stereotyped movements

reticular formation: diffuse web-like structure; filtering pathway of the central nervous system. Prioritizes flow for selective unconscious attention.

seizure: sudden firing of nerve cells in the brain resulting in a response ranging from severe, total body muscle spasms to a state of fogginess. Often can be controlled by medication

sensory defensiveness: avoidance to sensations; emotional behavior that is unpredictable may result when forced to participate

sensory systems: a complex network of nerve pathways designed to decode a variety of sensory stumuli

skill: ability to do something

space visualization: ability to perceive the relationship of a shape to the space surrounding it and to change the shape's positioning in the mind without touching it. Mental manipulation of objects in space

special education: services provided through the school system to mentally, physically, or emotionally impaired children, in order to provide the best educational opportunity possible

speech and language therapy: therapy aimed at evaluating and helping children overcome language disorders through concept and language development, muscle control and coordination, etc.

stereognosis: sensation of being able to identify objects through the sense of touch (without looking) by shape, weight, size

stimulation: therapy technique to increase the child's wanting or ability to do something; to provide the child with sensory or movement experiences

supine: lying on the back

symmetrical tonic neck reflex (STNR): a reflex in which when the head is bent forward the arms bend and legs straighten; when the head is bent backward the arms straighten and legs bend

tactile: referring to the sense of touch

tactile defensiveness: a disorder in which a child interprets tactile stimulation or kinds of touch in an unusual manner, such as complaining that a light touch hurts, that a firm touch tickles. The child might try to avoid hugging, hand holding, different textures of food, and so forth.

trunk: the body, not including the arms, legs, and head

trunk control: ability to keep the trunk steady or control its movement

vestibular: referring to the sensory system responsible for interpreting movement of the body in space

Wilbarger Approach to Treating Sensory Defensiveness: a specific technique in which a particular device is used to help the brain learn to reinterpret sensory input so that it is not offensive to the system. This is accomplished with a timed regimen of pressure touch followed immediately by quick compressions and a daily routine of moving, using muscles and joints to push, pull, lift, carry, tug, etc. This protocol must be followed as taught and must be supervised by a therapist who has been trained in this area.

visual discrimination: ability to match or determine exact characteristics of two forms when one of the forms is among similar forms

visual perception: the capacity to interpret or give meaning to what is seen; recognition, insight, and interpretation at the higher levels of the central nervous system to what is seen; i.e. the process of seeing, organizing and understanding what has been seen

visual memory: ability to remember what has been seen

visual-spatial relationships: ability to determine the part of a form that is going in a different direction

visual-form constancy: ability to see a form and find that form even though the form may be smaller, larger, rotated, reversed, and/or hidden

visual-sequential memory: ability to remember for immediate recall a series of forms from among a separate series of forms

visual figure-ground: ability to perceive a form visually, and to find this form hidden in a conglomerated ground of matter

visual closure: ability to determine, from among four incomplete forms, the one that is the same as the completed form

Bibliography

Abraham, Michael. (2002). *Addressing Learning Differences - Sensory Integration*, McGraw Hill, New York.

Anderson, E., and Emmons P. (1996). *Unlocking the Mysteries of Sensory Dysfunction*, Future Horizons, 721 W. Abram St., Arlington, TX 76013 (800) 489-0727 www.futurehorizons-autism.com

Advocate. *The Newsletter of the Autism Society of America*. Autism Society of America. www.autism-society.org

Alliance for Childhood. (2000). *Fools Gold: A Critical Look at Computers in Childhood*. Edited by Colleen Cordes and Edward Miller. www.allianceforchildhood.net

Attwood, Tony. (1998). *Asperger's Syndrome: A Guide for Parents and Professionals*. Jessica Kingsley Publishers.

Attwood, Tony. (2004). *Exploring Feelings – Cognitive Behavior Therapy to Manage ANGER*. www.futurehorizons-autism.com

Arvedson, Joan C. and Brodsky, Linda. (2001). *Pediatric Swallowing and Feeding: Assessment and Management* (Dysphagia Series). Singular; 2nd Edition.

Audette, LouAnne, OTR, Karson, Anne, OTR. (1998). *Getting it Write. A remedial handwriting program designed for groups of children to improve their handwriting skills*. The Abilities Center. www.theabilitiescenter.com

Autism Digest Magazine. Source of Information for Parents and Professionals. Click on Resource Center. www.futurehorizons-autism.com

Ayres, A.J. (1979). *Sensory Integration and the Child*. Los Angeles: Western Psychological Services, 12031 Wilshire Blvd., 90025-1251.

Bennett, Steve and Ruth. (2002). *365 TV Free Activities You Can Do With Your Child*. Adams Media Corporation, Avon, Massachusetts.

Barron, J., and Barron, S. (1992). *There's A Boy In Here*. New York: Simon & Schuster.

Benbow, Mary, MS, OTR. (1999). *Loops and Other Groups; A Kinesthetic Writing System*. Psychological Corporation. Check www.amazon.com and/or www.allegromedical.com

Beckman, Debra A. (2002-2005). *Oral Motor Interventions*. www.beckmanoral-motor.com

Berk, Laura E. (2004). *Awakening Children's Minds: How Parents and Teachers Can Make a Difference*. Oxford University Press; New Ed edition.

Biel, Lindsey; Peske, Nancy. (2005). *Raising a Sensory Smart Child: The Definitive Handbook for Helping Your Child with Sensory Integration Issues*. Penguin (Non-Classics).

Bickert, Grace. (2004). *Including the Special Needs Child. Activities to Help All Students Grow and Learn*. Can be ordered from Achievement Products for Children. www.specialkidszone.com (800) 373-4699

Bissell, J.; Fisher, J.; Owens, C., and Polycyn, P. (1998) *Sensory Motor Handbook: A Guide Implementing and Modifying activities in the Classroom*. Sensory Integration International. www.sensoryint.com Sensory Integration Dysfunction – Sensory Integration International – Request for list of trained therapists in your area and/or use as gateway to more information. www.kid-power.org/sid.html

Broadley, M.E., (1986). *Your Natural Gifts. How to Recognize and Develop Them for Success and Self-fulfillment*. McLean, BA, 22101: EMP Publications.

Bryson, Tily, McKay, Swalling, Parshin, and Parrish. (1988). *Electric Bread: A Bread Machine Activity Book for Kids*. Innovative Cooking Enterprises, I.C.E., Inc., Anchorage, Alaska.

Bryte, Kathy, OTR/L. (1996). *Classroom Intervention for the School-Based Therapist – An Integrated Model*. Therapy Skill Builders, 555 Academic Ct., San Antonio, TX 78204-2498.

Bundy, Anita; Lane, Shelly, Murray, Elizabeth. (2002). *Sensory Integration Theory and Practice*, Second Edition. FA Davis Co., Philadelphia, PA 19103. www.fadavis.com

Campbell, Don. (2000). *The Mozart Effect for Children: Awakening Your Child's Mind, Health, and Creativity with Music*. Human Sciences Press Inc., New York, NY. www.mozarteffect.com

Carper, Jean. (2000). *Your Miracle Brain*. HarperCollins Publishers Inc., 10 E. 53rd St., New York, NY.

Christiansen, Charles; Matuska, Kathleen. (2004). *Ways of Living. Adaptive Strategies for Special Needs*. American Occupational Association Press www.aota.org

Davalos, Sandra R. (1999). *Making Sense of Art: Sensory-Based Art Activities for Children with Autism*, Asperger Syndrome and other Pervasive Developmental Disorders. Autism Asperger Publishing Co. www.asperger.net

DeNinno, Joanne P., Gill, Kim A, Rowland, Rick. (1997). *"Can Do" Oral-Motor Fun and Games*. Super Duper Publications, PO Box 24997, Greenville, South Carolina, 29616.

Dennison, Paul E., Ph.D; Dennison, Gail E. (1989) *Brain Gym Teacher's Edition*, Edu-Kinesthetics, Inc., Ventura, CA. www.braingym.com

Dunn, Winnie, PhD., OTR, FAOTA. (2002). *Infant/Toddler Sensory Profile*. www.SensoryProfile.com

Dyer, Wayne. *The Power of Intention*. (2004). Hay House, Inc. Carlsbad, CA.

Ernsperger, Tania, Ph.D., Stegen-Hanson, OTR/L. (2004). *Just Take A Bite*. Future Horizons. www.futurehorizons-autism.com

Gardner, Morrison F. (1995). *Test of Visual Motor Skills, Revised*. Psychological and Educational Publications, Inc., Hydesville, CA.

Goleman, D. (1995). *Emotional Intelligence*. New York: Bantam.

Grandin, Temple. (1986). *Emergence: Labeled Autistic*. Warner Books.

Grandin, Temple. (1996). *Thinking in Pictures and Other Reports from My Life with Autism*. New York: Vintage Books, A Division of Random House, Inc.

Grandin, Temple; Barron, Sean. (2005). *Unwritten Rules of Social Relationships*. Future Horizons. www.futurehorizons-autism.com

Greenspan, S., MD. (1995). *The Challenging Child*. New York: Addison-Wesley. (2004). *Greenspan Social-Emotional Growth Chart*. www.PsychCorp.com

Gurian, Michael, et al. (2001). *Boys and Girls Learn Differently!: A Guide for Teachers and Parents*. Jossey-Bass, San Francisco, CA.

Haldy, M.; Haack, L. (1995). *Making It Easy: Sensorimotor Activities at Home and School*. Tucson: Therapy Skill Builders.

Hallowell, Edward M.; Ratey, John. (1995). *Driven to Distraction: Recognizing and Coping with Attention Deficit Disorder from Childhood Through Adulthood*. Touchstone; reprint edition.

Hannaford, Carla, Ph.D. (1995). *Smart Moves: Why Learning is Not All in Your Head*. Great River Books.

Hannaford, Carla, Ph.D. (1997). *The Dominance Factor; How Knowing Your Dominant Eye, Ear, Brain, hand, & Foot Can Improve Your Learning*. Great River Books.

Heller, Sharon. (2002). *Too Loud, Too Bright, Too Fast, Too Tight. What to do if you are sensory defensive in an over stimulating world*. HarperCollins Publishers, New York, NY.

Heiberger, Heiniger-White (2002). *S'Cool Moves for Learning*. Integrated Learning Press. Available from Achievement Products for Children www.specialkidszone.com

Hirsh-Pasek, Kathy; Eyer, Diane; Michnick Golinkoff, Roberta. (2003). *Einstein Never Used Flash Cards: How Our Children Really Learn—And Why They Need to Play More and Memorize Less*. Rodale Books. www.rodalestore.com

Hubert, Bill. Bal-A-Vis-X. (2001). *Rhythmic Balance/Auditory/Vision Exercises for Brain and Brain-body Integration*. Bal-A-Vis-X, Inc., bill@bal-a-vis-x.com

Klein, Marshia, MEd, OTR/L; Delaney, PhD, RD. (1994). *Feeding and Nutrition for the Child with Special Needs*. www.mealtimenotions.com

Knickerbocker, Barbara, M. (1992). *A Holistic Approach to the Treatment of Learning Disorders*. Charles B. Slack, Inc., Thorofare, NJ.

Kramer, P.; Hinojosa, J. (1993). *Frames of Reference for Pediatric Occupational Therapy*. Baltimore, MD., Williams & Wilkins.

Kranowitz, Carol, MA (1998). *The Out-of-Sync Child: Recognizing and Coping with Sensory Integration Dysfunction*. New York, NY. The Berkley Publishing Group.

Kranowitz, Carol, MA. (1995). *101 Activities for Kids in Tight Spaces. St. Martin's Griffin*. Published by arrangement with Skylight Press, NY.

Kranowitz, Carol, MA. (2003). *The Out-of-Sync Child Has Fun*. The Berkley Publishing Group, NY.

Lewis, Lisa. (1998). *Special Diets for Special Kids*. Future Horizons. www.futurehorizons-autism.com

Landy, Joanne M; Burridge, Keith R. (2000). *Ready-to-Use Fine Motor Skills & Handwriting Activities for Young Children*. Center for Applied Research in Education.

Levine, Mel, MD. (2002). *A Mind at a Time*. Simon & Schuster.

Levine, Mel, MD. (2005). *Ready or Not, Here Life Comes*. Simon & Schuster

McCall, Renee, MS.; Craft, Diane H. (2000). *Moving with a Purpose*. Human Kinetics, Ill. Available from Achievement Products for Children. www.specialkidszone.com

McCall, Renee and Craft, Diane, Ph.D. (2004). *Purposeful Play: Early Childhood Movement Activities on a Budget*. Human Kinetics Publishers.

Miller, Lucy J., Ph.D., OTR, FAOTA *Miller Function & Participation Scales* (2006). Harcourt Assessment, Inc. Available at www.PsychCorp.com

Morris, Suzanne Evans, CCC, SP, Marcia Dunn Klein, MEd, OTR/L. (2001). *Pre-Feeding Skills: A Comprehensive Resource for Mealtime Development* 2nd Edition www.mealtimenotions.com

Morris, Lisa Rappaport; Schultz, Linda. (1989). *Creative Play Activities for Children with Disabilities. A Resource book for Teachers and Parents*. 2nd Edition. Developed by the Joseph P. Kennedy, Jr., Foundation. www.humankinetics.com

Myles, Brenda Smith; Cook, Katherine; Miller, Nancy; Rinner, Louann; Robbins, Lisa. (2000). *Asperger Syndrome and Sensory Issues*. Autism Asperger Publishing Co. www.asperger.net

Olsen, Jan Z., OTR. (1998). *Handwriting Without Tears*. (2005). Readiness Program. Get Set for School, etc. www.hwtears.com

Page, Christine, MD; Howard, Martha, MD. (1998). *Subtle Energy Medicine – A course for licensed health professionals*. Sponsored by the International Conference on the Psychology of Health, Immunity, and Disease. **National Institute for the Clinical Application of Behavioral Medicine** www.nicabm.com

Palladino, Lucy Jo. (1999). *Dreamers, Discoverers, & Dynamos* (formerly *The Edison Trait*). The Ballantine Publishing Group/division of Random House, Inc. NY. www.randomhouse.com

Pruitt, David B. (1999). *Your Child: What Every Parent Needs to Know: What's Normal, What's Not, and When to Seek Help*. Ed, American Academy of Child & Adolescent Psychiatry. HarperCollins Publishers, Inc.

Reisman, J. & Hanschu, B. (1992). *Sensory Integration Inventory-Revised for Individuals with Developmental Disabilities: User's Guide*, Hugo, MN; PDP Press.

Restak, Richard, MD. (2001). *Mozart's Brain and the Fighter Pilot: Unleashing Your Brain's Potential*. Three Rivers Press, New York. www.rodalestore.com

Restak, Richard, MD. (2004). *the new brain; HOW THE MODERN AGE IS REWIRING YOUR MIND*. Holtzbrinck Publishers. www.rodalestore.com

Robbins, Anthony. (1997). *Unlimited Power*. Free Press, Reprint Edition. www.anthonyrobbins.com

Rodman, Karen. (2003). *Asperger's Syndrome and Adults...Is Anyone Listening?* Jessica Kinsley Publishers.

Satter, Ellyn, RD, ACSW. (2005). *Secrets of Feeding a Healthy Family*. Kelcy Press. www.mealtimenotions.com

Schlessinger, Dr. Laura. (2000). *Parenthood by Proxy-Don't Have Them If You Won't Raise Them*. HarperCollins Publishers Inc. www.drlaura.com

Shellenberger, Sherry, OTR; Williams, Mary Sue, OTR. (1996). *"How Does Your Engine Run?" A Leader's Guide to the Alert Program for Self Regulation* and (2001) *Take Five: Staying Alert at Home and School*. TherapyWorks, Inc. www.alertprogram.com

Schneider, Catherine Chemin, OTR. (2006). *Sensory Secrets: How to Jump-Start Learning in Children*. The Concerned Group, Inc. www.theconcernedgroup.com www.sensorysecrets.com Book can be ordered at (800) 447-4332.

Silberg, Jackie. *Games to Play with Babies* (2001); *Games to Play with Toddlers* (2002); *and Games to Play with Two Year Olds* (2002). Available from www. beyondplay.com

Snowdon, David. (2002). *Aging with Grace. What the Nun Study Teaches Us About Leading Longer, Healthier and More Meaningful Lives*. Bantam

Sornson, Bob (Editor) (2001). *Preventing Early Learning Failure*: Association for Supervision and Curriculum Development.

Sunbeck, Deborah, Ph.D. (1996). *Infinity Walk. Preparing your mind to learn*. Jalmar Press. www.jalmarpress.com or www.proedinc.com

Sunbeck, Deborah, Ph.D. (2002). *The Complete Infinity Walk*. Leonardo Foundation Press. www.leonardofoundationpress.com

Taylor, Arlene, PhD.; Brewer, Dr. Gene; Nash, Michelle. (2003). *MindWaves*. The Concerned Group, Inc. www.arlenetaylor.org and/or www.theconcernedgroupinc. com Book can be ordered at (800) 447- 4332.

Trott, M.C.; Laurel, M.; Windeck, S.L. (1993). *SenseAbilities: Understanding Sensory Integration*. Tucson, AZ Therapy Skill Builders.

Vitale, Meister B., (1982). *Unicorns Are Real. A Right-Brained Approach to Learning*. Rolling Hills Estates, CA 90274 www.jalmarpress.com

Walsh, David, Ph.D. (1996). *Physicians Guide to Media Violence*. American Medical Association. www.mediafamily.org

Waltz, Mitzi. (1999). *Pervasive Developmental Disorders: Finding a Diagnosis and Getting Help*. OReilly & Associates, Inc.

Wilbarger, P.; Wilbarger, J. (1991). *Introduction to Sensory Defensiveness: An Intervention Guide for Children 2-12*. Santa Barbara, CA. Avanti Educational Programs. (818) 782-7366 Fax: (818) 989-7826.

Wiley, Liane Holliday. (1999). *Pretending to be Normal: Living with Asperger's Syndrome*. Jessica Kingsley Publishers.

Yack, Ellen; Sutton Shirley; Aquilla, Paula. (2003). *Building Bridges Through Sensory Integration*, 2nd Edition. Sensory Resources. www.sensoryresources.com

Young, S.B.; Keplinger, L. (1988). *Movement is Fun: A Preschool Movement Program*. Torrance, CA. Sensory Integration International. www.sensoryint.com

Zysk, Veronica; Notbohm, Ellen. (2004). *1001 Great Ideas for Teaching and Raising Children with Autism Spectrum Disorders*. Future Horizons. www. futurehorizons-autism.com

Endnotes

[1]Carper, Jean, *Your Miracle Brain*, p. 30-32

[2]Hannaford, Carla, *Smart Moves: Why Learning Is Not All in Your Head*, p. 96.

[3]Fisher, Anne G., Murray, Elizabeth A., and Bundy, Anita C, *Sensory Integration Theory and Practice*, p. 77-78.

[4]Schlessinger, Dr. Laura, *Parenthood by Proxy*, p. 34.

[5]Schlessinger, p. 212.

[6]Hannaford, p. 48.

[7]Williams, Mary Sue, and Shellenberger, Sherry, *How Does Your Engine Run? A Leader's Guide to The Alert Program for Self-Regulation*, p. 5, Foreword, and Preface.

How to use the Foundational Skills Inventory

The Foundational Skills Inventory is a tool to help you "picture" the areas of need in development that might be present for any given person. Beginning at the bottom of the page, the Inventory represents steps to the top, where academics would be found.

The goal is to darken out anything that is not true for the person being assessed. Therefore the Inventory had to be written in a "problematic" format. Please realize that this format is necessary for the Inventory to be effective. The color combination is designed to make the levels distinct and easy to read.

The Foundational Skills Inventory was designed to quickly and efficiently indicate any areas that may need further attention. It is my hope that it will be extremely helpful in creating goals that will facilitate the learning process.

Quick Guide to Using the Inventory:

- Start at the bottom of the page
- Circle statements that are true
- Darken out what is not true
- If in doubt about an item, skip it
- View current foundation for learning
- Assess need for "Sensory Diet"
- Create goals that take sensory development into consideration